Everything I Ever Needed To Know About Life... I Learned In Prison

A Memoir

Kevin Gilford

Gilford Press

Contents

To all the amazing women in my life,
Mom, Cindy, Nobalee, Valene, Chelsea
and a special thank you to Lauren my editor (and task master!)

*THE MOVING FINGER
WRITES; AND HAVING
WRIT,*

*MOVES ON: NOR ALL THY
PIETY NOR WIT*

*SHALL LURE IT BACK TO
CANCEL HALF A LINE,*

*NOR ALL THY TEARS WASH
OUT A WORD OF IT.*

-Omar Khayyam

Foreward

The names in this narrative have been changed not only to protect the innocent and guilty alike, but also because for the most part, I can't remember the names. The faces and events are crystallized in my memory as if these things happened yesterday. The names, not so much.

I'd like to also point out that everyone's experiences vary, and mine are unique to me. Many of the rules, written and unwritten alike, vary from prison to prison. Each time I was moved to a new joint, it was like learning how to do time all over again.

My memories that I impart to you in the following pages are true to the best of my knowledge, yet as it is with any story, acting participants often have varying versions. The effect they had on me, the way they made me feel and ultimately shaped my life is what is most important. So, if anyone should care to dispute the facts, I would not disagree with them. The results on me, however, cannot be argued.

I've been toying with the idea of writing this book for years, and had it not been for the constant encouragement from friends, family, and mostly from my wife, Cindy, it may not have ever happened. It's been exactly three years since I began, writing this on my phone as I drank my morning coffee, while in waiting rooms, and in the parking lot before going in to work. I hope you'll find inspiration, comedy, and maybe some thought provoking anecdotes?

As for the title of this book, admittedly it is somewhat misleading. I had wonderful caring parents who did the best they could to teach me right from wrong, so I have only me to blame for the path I took. And oh, what a path it's been.

I KNOW WHAT I'M DOING

"Kevin always has to learn things the hard way." I must have heard my mother utter that phrase a thousand times, from my earliest memories to the not-so-distant past. It's true. If the title of this book isn't testament enough, there's a popular family story my mom loves to tell about me as a wee lad of four or five years old.

We lived in northern California in the early 1970's, a time when we kids would be out the front door at the break of day riding bikes, building forts, and basically running wild all over creation with little to no adult supervision. Once the streetlights came on, that was our signal that it was time to return home.

On this particular occasion, it must have been early in our day's adventures because the sun was shining bright, and we had yet to venture past our front yard. We had a beautiful ranch home, boasting a wide, perfectly manicured lawn that was the envy of all the parents on our cul-de-sac. Set on the back corner of that lawn, at the edge of the house, was a bottlebrush shrub with bright red blooms that was a main attraction for honeybees in the area. It was there that I happened upon my brother Todd and one of his friends from the neighborhood. They were engaged in the serious and intense work of puffing plumes of baby powder onto the bees as they visited the flowering bush.

"Hey guys, whatcha doing?" I inquired as I came on the scene, trying to insert myself into their festivities. "None of your business," Todd snapped as he puffed another bee. He was taciturn at best, reluctant to allow me to do so much as orbit in his

vicinity, let alone join in his fun. He was four years my senior, and I idolized him completely. No amount of Todd's surliness could dissuade me. "We're marking these bees, so we know which ones have already been here when they come back,' the neighborhood kid Gregg replied as he puffed his own target.

I stood mesmerized as I watched them at their craft. The jets of gleaming white powder shooting from the caps of their travel sized bottles, coating the butts and wings of their prey the way my mother would coat a cake with powdered sugar.

"Let me! I wanna try!" I squealed. "Forget it you little turd, you're too little for this," Todd chided me. I can't be sure if it was a mother's intuition or my high-pitched wailing that brought her to the window, but nevertheless, there she was in an instant. "Kevin, you stay away from those bees! You'll get stung!" Todd and Gregg, realizing that their clandestine operation had been exposed, handed me their bottles of baby powder without a word and walked away.

I ignored both their departure and my mom's warnings, delighted to be left to carry on the mission my elders had begun. With a bottle in each hand, I took up my position at the bush and began my double-fisted assault. The subtle nuances of puffing a gentle cloud onto the bees was beyond my comprehension. I blasted them point blank with all the force the bottles would allow. "Kevin Trent

Gilford, you're gonna get stung! I told you to quit harassing those bees!" My mother's admonishment came again from the window, more urgently this time. It was then that I first uttered the phrase that would define my life for the next thirty years: "I know what I'm doing!" I yelled back at her like a snarky brat. The bees at that moment mounted their retaliation, and their attack was blitzkrieg in nature! Their stingers found their marks in my legs, torso, and neck simultaneously!

I immediately began the instinctual dance of running around in circles, screaming, and flailing my arms in panic. Mom came bursting out the front door and swiftly corralled me into submission on the front lawn, where she took to swatting the bees with her bare hands. Once the onslaught had subsided, mom ushered me into the house for some first aid. I was doing that pathetic thing kids do near the end of a good cry where I was sniveling and muttering incoherent phrases while sucking in quick gasps of air through my nostrils and mouth. There was another jolt of fear when a lone bee came buzzing out of the folds of my shirt as Mom helped me pull it off, over my head. My ear-splitting shrieks nearly deafened us both in the echo chamber that was our bathroom. I needn't have worried; mom deftly dispatched this one with the same speed and brutality as she did its comrades in the front yard.

My mother lovingly plucked out stingers, applied mercurochrome and gently bandaged my sores. All while calmly trying to explain why kids should listen to their parents, and how it's for our protection and not to stop our enjoyment, blah, blah, blah.

I don't recall exactly what I said as she helped me back into my shirt, but it must have been some rationale as to why it was a fluke that I was attacked by bees, and that I really *did* know what I was doing, because her face pinched in an expression of complete incomprehension. She handed me back my plastic bottles of baby powder, "Fine! Go out there and get some more bees!" She turned on her heels and left me standing there with fresh tears welling in my eyes and a bottle of baby powder clutched in each hand. So, you see, it wasn't that I came from a loveless home, or parents that didn't try teaching me wrong from right. I just always had to learn things the hard way.

Chapter Two

I ALWAYS GOT CAUGHT

When I tell you I have always been bad at not getting caught, I do mean "always!" When I was just a boy, not old enough to be in school yet. I began poking things with a number two pencil out of boredom which then became a compulsion. I enjoyed the way it felt when the point of the pencil pierced into an object. First came the carpet. It made a satisfying snap when the tip of my pencil punched through the backing of the carpet and into the padding underneath where it came to a cushioned stop. About thirty pokes on any one surface was all that could hold my attention before I searched out a new target. I poked the bedding a few times. Not as great as the carpeting; this was worth only a few pokes of my pencil. Then came the curtains. "Lame!" Since the curtains were attached at only one end, there wasn't enough resistance for my pencil to do its work. I spotted the tiny checkerboard pattern of the screen peeking from behind the curtains on the other side of the window, "Aha," I thought, "this would make for some good poking!" And it sure did. I opened the window and gave it an overhand thrust. I heard the snap of the mesh breaking as my missile found its mark, and the feel of the pencil coming to a stop as the resistance overcame my force was satisfying as well. This must have amused me for a good fifty pokes all over the screen before I lost interest and found some other way to destroy property.

My poke fest had been a distant memory to me by the time I received my spanking for the offense, which hardly seemed fair. No statute of limitations in my father's monarchy, apparently. He took me to my room, pulled back the curtains and asked me why I had done such a thing. I immediately started bawling and blubbering incoherent words to defend my actions, which bought me no leniency whatsoever. Pity, this tactic always worked on my mother. He closed the curtains, took me over his knee and gave me one hundred brutal lashes! Okay, it was probably more like five firm swats across the buttocks, but I swear it felt like a hundred! He left me sniveling as I lay upon my bed. He closed the door on his way out, and I heard his footsteps retreat down the hall. I waited a few extra moments to be sure he was out of earshot, then began a quiet verbal retaliation of the things I didn't have the courage to say to his face. "Dad's a fuck-ass!" (A hybrid phrase I coined out of the worst cuss words I knew at the time). "He's a butthole," I continued. My diatribe was cut short when I heard the front door slam, followed by heavy footfalls heading up the hall! My door swung open, and my father's hulking form filled the doorway.

If I thought the first round of spankings felt like a hundred lashes, this bout felt like a thousand! "You don't ever talk about your father like that, you understand me?" He admonished me as he delivered the blows across my ass. How the hell he even heard me was beyond my comprehension!

Once he felt like I'd had enough, he stormed out of my room once again. This time I listened carefully to be sure I heard him stomp down the hallway and slam the front door on his way out. It was difficult to hear over my sniveling, not to mention my thundering heartbeats, so I waited an extra few minutes before I resumed my litany of curses towards my father. I was extra smart about it this time. First, I was even more quiet than my first round. Also, I huddled up on my bed, against the wall under the window so I was as far from the door to my room as possible, and I buried my face in a pillow before I began my tirade. "Fucking, fucker ass! Butthole..." Not two phrases in before I heard the front door slamming once again, and the heavy footsteps of doom heading towards my door! The familiar scene played out once again with my back side getting tanned while my father lectured me on not taking his name in vain. Again, he left in a huff, while I lay folded over in the fetal position upon my bed, gasping for air through a snot—filled nose, and over my spittle—laced lips. I cowered in a ball on my bed for a little while as I searched my young feeble brain for answers as to how he had heard my rants, and also on what my next course of action should be. I concluded that I couldn't reside under this oppression any longer. I was going to run away! I sprang into action, grabbing what I would need for life on the road. Some of my favorite Hot Wheels, Star Trek action figures, and a sweater in case it got cold.

Ready for my escape, I kneeled upon the bed and flung back the curtains, ready to climb through the window. There, to my utter shock, was my father, framed perfectly in the window as he worked at repairing the screen. The window had already been opened, so I heard him clearly when he spoke in a calm and measured tone,

"Going somewhere?" I suddenly had total clarity of all that had transpired. "Nope, just getting some fresh air," I replied before making a big production of taking a deep breath and drawing the curtains shut.

Some years later when I was in the fifth grade, I was approached by my classmate Mark about selling plug chewing tobacco to our brethren on the playground at recess. This was my introduction to the entrepreneurial lifestyle that I would draw upon in my drug dealing phase of life not many years later.

"Hey Kevin, you want to make some money?" he asked me that fateful day. "Sure, what do I have to do?" I asked. He pulled out the package of tobacco that looked like a brick of mulch. "You just tear off a little hunk like this and sell it to dudes on the playground at recess," he told me as he separated a wad about an inch in diameter.

"What the hell is it?" I asked.

"Chewing tobacco, ain't you never heard of it?" I hadn't heard of it, but I thought I'd look stupid if I said so. "Oh yeah, I just never saw this brand before," was my reply. The deal was to sell the product and split the money at the end of the day.

It sounded like a good deal, so I took him up on it since it took almost no effort on my part, and what seemed to be little risk to me. He would bring the tobacco to school each morning and tear me off half of the brick. We would go our separate ways and wait for our clients to approach us. I'd only had to inquire if anyone was looking to buy some on my first day. After that, just as with selling drugs, the product sold itself. Kids would get a small pinch of the goods in exchange for 25 cents. If I sold my entire inventory, I would net about two dollars which I split with my supplier Mark. Since he supplied the goods, it seemed a fair arrangement.

Our empire had been running smoothly for the better part of a week before it all came crashing down. Mark and I shared Mrs. Brazil's classroom and sat a few rows apart from one another. It was during class that I noticed Mark trying to get my attention. Once he had it, he tried to convey what he wanted by mouthing words that I couldn't decipher and motioning with his hands that could've meant, "come here," or "give me something," I couldn't tell which. What I could tell was that he was attracting the attention of everyone in the room, including Mrs. Brazil! I slightly raised my hand and made a "pump the brakes motion" to chill him out, then made a point of completely ignoring him for the remainder of the class. Though I could see out of the corner of my eye, he continued to try and draw my attention.

I don't recall why, but at some point during the class we were allowed out of our seats to meander around. Mark made a beeline straight to me. "Dude, I need the stuff," he began urgently, "Whatever you have left, I need it!" I wanted to tell him to chill out until recess, but before I could utter a word Mrs. Brazil intervened. "What's going on here, boys?" She asked in a firm and authoritative voice. Mark, that little shit, tried to turn and walk away, but was suddenly stopped and spun around by Mrs. Brazil as she latched her fingers around his upper arm. I must have given myself away as I instinctively reached for my front pocket momentarily before checking my movement and dropping my hand back by my side. "What's in your pocket, Mr. Gilford?" she demanded. "N-n-n-nothing," I stammered. She just raised an eyebrow and held out her hand. The jig was up. I pulled out the wad of tobacco which was wrapped in a piece of loose-leaf binder paper and dropped it in her hand. She had an incredulous look on her face as she poked at the paper with an index finger. "What is it?" she asked. I quickly tried to formulate a clever response that could get us out of this mess, but before my synapses could fire, Mark, in an attempt to exonerate himself, blew the whole thing by exclaiming, "Chewing tobacco! What are you doing with that?" I could see from the face she pulled that Mrs. Brazil wasn't buying it. "Both of you, to the principal's office."

Mark wasted no time in spilling the beans about our enterprise to the principal, Mr. Mimeo. If he thought it would buy him clemency, he was mistaken. We were both suspended for the remainder of the week.

One more of my brilliant case studies in getting caught was when I came home drunk at the tender age of thirteen.

There was a woman named Ginger who lived next door and used to indulge my brother and me with beer and grass (what us old timers used to call marijuana). It was all done in an attempt to seduce my older brother, which worked perfectly. I don't really blame either of them. After all, it's every young man's fantasy to be pursued by an attractive older woman, and for her, Todd was a handsome fucker at sixteen. He must have thought so as well because he often told himself so while brushing his golden mane in the mirror, "what a babe."

At any rate, Todd and I were over at Ginger's place under the guise of babysitting her two young children. In truth, I was sitting the kids while she and my brother were up to hijinks in the bedroom. Until this night there had just been a lot of flirting between those two, and Ginger would monitor my intake of alcohol. This night, however, it had progressed to the next level, and since the tryst in the bedroom lasted several hours, I had plenty of time to overindulge. By the time they emerged from the love nest I was completely hammered. I remember stumbling home and announcing to my mother that I'd suddenly come down with the flu and was heading to bed. It seemed like a plausible excuse at the time.

At some point during the night as I lay in bed, fighting a bad case of the spins, I overheard my mother on the phone with my dad, discussing my condition. They had been divorced for several years at this point but maintained a very amicable relationship. Any worry of facing my father's wrath dissolved from the forefront of my mind during my many trips to worship at the porcelain altar, where I made all the usual professions to God about never drinking again if he could just spare me this suffering.

At some point I finally found the sweet release of sleep, but it wasn't to last. It was still dark when I heard my father calling to me in that deep booming voice of his, "Kevin Trent, wake up son, it's time to go. No school for you today, we're going fishing." Despite my protestations, he wrangled me out of bed and into my clothes. Before I knew it, we were at his house where he made me eat the disgusting breakfast he'd prepared for me of runny eggs and burnt toast. I only recall events in flashes: hooking up the boat trailer to the truck, stopping at a market for ice and supplies, and the long drive down to the boat ramp. What I do remember with painful clarity, was finding myself in that little aluminum boat, rocking on the choppy waves of the Sacramento River, fighting back my nausea, and wishing for it all to end.

We trolled up and down that waterway, bumping and rolling over the whitecaps as the trees along the shoreline cast light and shadows across my blurred vision. As the dawn approached, my stomach was even more tumultuous than the water, and by noon, with the sun beating down on us, I had expelled every last drop of liquid from my guts over the side of our vessel. "Dad, I need something to drink," I asked pathetically. Dad made a grand gesture of opening the cooler which lay at his feet in the rear of the boat where he manned the outboard motor. "What's this?" he asked rhetorically, "I forgot to buy water or soda. Oh well, I guess one beer won't hurt." He pulled out a Natural Lite, popped the top and passed it to me. I can only imagine the look I gave him at the time, but it must have given him great satisfaction, because his smile was beaming.

He plied me with beer in that scorching California heat, bounced us over rolling waves and blew plumes of thick cigar smoke in my direction for the entirety of the day, but never made a single comment about my drinking, or punishment. It was understood, and we both knew I'd paid the price.

Chapter Three
DIARY OF A METH MAN

By the time I reached my second year of high school in 1986, I was flunking nearly all my classes. I must have had some form of ADD, because I just couldn't concentrate no matter how hard I tried. I distinctly recall giving myself pep talks about taking notes and paying attention just to find myself waking from daydreams halfway through every class I took.

This happened with such regularity that I never had a chance. I was so downtrodden that I eventually began to skip classes, more often than not. I would hang out at the railroad tracks that ran behind our school with my friends smoking pot and chewing tobacco, attending only the classes I was passing: metal shop, computer literacy and, oddly enough, science. I couldn't even get a passing grade in P.E.! I was a fat kid without an athletic bone in my body.

It was at this time that my father lost a yearlong battle with lung cancer. It's a tough thing for a kid to lose a parent, and for me I'd lost my rudder. My mother is the most kind, gentle and loving person on the planet, but fear of my father had been the only thing keeping me from completely flunking out of school.

I eventually fell far enough behind that I was sent to Ridgeview, a school that let students do work at their own pace in order to make up credits and hopefully be able to graduate with their class.

One day I had been hanging out with my brothers girlfriend Kat. We had cut through the woods that separated the trailer park I lived in from the strip mall where we were headed. Most likely to swipe shit from K-Mart since neither of us had any money. I didn't care what we were doing, I was just thrilled to be around her. Me and my friends were smitten with her. She had platinum dyed hair and big boobs. A teenage boy's fantasy.

She stopped at a secluded area in the woods and squatted down on a stump and pulled out a compact from her purse. I thought she was about to touch up her already heavy make-up, but instead she produced a glass vial and dumped a mound of white powder onto the mirror.

"What's that," I asked.

"Crank. Wanna try some?"

"Sure." Anything this chick did was cool in my book.

She chopped up two small lines with her school ID card and used a plastic straw to sniff up her line before handing the straw to me. "Just sniff it quickly like you've got a runny nose." She instructed me as she held the mirror up to my face. I did it just like she told me to, and it was love at first snort! Suddenly my mind and body were overtaken with an incredible feeling of energy and focus. I felt as if I had just woken from a foggy daydream, and now I was fully awake.

I did the drug as often as I could, I was bounding with creativity, which I loved because drawing and art were the only pleasures, I was passionate about.

Crank was an expensive drug, far too expensive for me to afford on my part time dishwasher's salary. Thankfully, I found that there was a high demand for it amongst my friends at school. I bought in bulk and parceled it out in quarter-gram increments which not only covered the cost of my own supply but put a few bucks in my pocket to boot.

Soon I was plowing through classes at school, sometimes finishing an entire course in one week. I would pick up a course packet, do the reading and all the material required, then hand it in and wait for it to be corrected. Then a teacher would give me a test on the subject, and bam! Just like that, another two credits made up.

I was devouring the information now that I could concentrate. I had found the magic pill, so to speak. I even began reading books for the first time in my life and enjoyed doing so. Books on the Holocaust, on the Old West, on ancient Rome. You name it, I read it and loved it. Where had this drug been all my life? I imagined this must be what everyone else—the kids who were doing well in school, excelling in sports, and generally leading happy productive lives—felt like without the drug. I felt as if I too now had access to what everyone else had naturally.

I began to lose weight and was able to buy a flashy sports car. To say my popularity was increasing would be an understatement. I had morals though. Even though the popular girls were now taking an interest in me, I shut them down cold whenever they tried flirting with me. If they didn't like me when I was a fat kid driving a Datsun, they couldn't have me now that I was slender and driving a Camaro! What was I thinking?!

Halfway through my junior year I was on track to graduate one year early. My meth-fueled focus was paying dividends when it suddenly became apparent to me that I was making more money than my mother, and she had raised two kids on those wages!

I dropped out of school completely to dedicate myself full time to dealing crank. My poor mother pleaded with me not to do it, and it broke her heart when I followed through with it. Before I left school, I signed up to go to automotive technician school after my eighteenth birthday, and a promise to keep that commitment was the only hope I left her of ever making something of myself. Little did she know I'd only promised to go to appease her and save her some micron of sorrow.

The best ratio I had found was to stay awake doing crank for three nights and then get one night's sleep. Unfortunately, once I didn't have to worry about school, the party nights began blending together and I would lose track of how many days I'd gone without sleep. When I did sleep, I could sleep for twenty-four hours or more without realizing it.

One time I woke up and saw it was six o clock, when my shift was supposed to start. I raced to work in what I thought was the twilight of night, only to arrive and find the restaurant closed. It was six in the morning, dawn. Funny how I hadn't noticed all the closed stores and lack of traffic along the way.

I lost my job at the restaurant soon after. Why had I kept it at all? I'm not sure, maybe to preserve the appearance of normality?

Losing that job may have been the first thing that the drug—which had given me so much at first—had taken away. Either way, at the time it seemed inconsequential.

I embraced the tweaker lifestyle wholeheartedly after that. Selling and doing lots of crank. Partying every night and day, having lots of sex, and shooting endless games of pool at my favorite flophouse. We shot so many games of pool on that table that it had to be re-felted every few months! I felt as though I was living the life of a rock star without ever having picked up an instrument.

I made it to the top of the food chain in our culture for a time, manufacturing the drug under the tutelage of long-time cooks. It was thrilling to be in that position, and I found all kinds of ways to justify it to myself.

I would never sell it to kids, junkies, or to anyone I thought wasn't being responsible with it. Of course, I was just a kid myself, so I must've thought 'kids' meant someone under the age of sixteen.

I despised the use of needles, and would openly shame anyone who used them, refusing to sell it to them, or even associate with them. Junkies I felt could not be trusted because they would do anything for another fix. They would steal, lie and even narc you out if it came to that.

As for people not using responsibly, well that one seemed to be on a sliding scale. My definition let us say, evolved. As time went on, I found all sorts of ways to justify the bending of my morals, especially if it suited my needs at the time.

Along the way I picked up the nickname *Danger*. A bunch of us were partying at a favorite flophouse, shooting pool, talking shit, and doing endless lines of crank for so many days in a row I'd lost count (as was known to happen). At some point Eddie, the main cook and de facto boss of our little operation had become irritated with Jerry, one of the guests. Eddie pulled me aside and told me, "You gotta get rid of this guy." Being the good soldier and subordinate that I was, I quickly devised a plan to carry out the order. I enlisted the help of our comrade Jimbo, who told Jerry he was going on a secret mission with us.

It's hard to describe the culture of a group of meth-heads. We're both paranoid yet ready to join in on any shenanigans, especially those at the behest of a cook or boss if you will. So, it was no trouble convincing Jerry to load up in the back of my car on this clandestine operation.

Now unbeknownst to me or the others who were there when Eddie was telling me to *get rid of Jerry*, a young girl named Chara had been listening in from a nearby hallway, and she'd taken the words to mean a completely different thing than what I, or the others had in mind. So, when I began to pull out of the driveway with Jerry in the backseat and Jimbo seated next to me in the front, Chara came running out of the house screaming, "Danger! Danger! Danger!" Thinking poor Jerry was about to be murdered.

Chara was a hardcore tweaker known for erratic behavior, so I thought nothing of it, and continued on my way. "Your name is Danger?" Jerry inquired from the rear of the car. Before I could offer a reply, Jimbo answered, "Yeah. Isn't that right, Danger?" I was truly confused at the time, so I merely shrugged my shoulders and proceeded with the mission.

I drove us an hour and a half into the rural mountains of northern California until I came to a gas station. This was 1987 so I pumped the gas from the lone pump that stood out front of this ramshackle looking little place and asked Jerry to go in to pay for it and buy us some beers. A reasonable request since Jimbo and I were underage. I handed Jerry a twenty-dollar bill and waited until he was inside the store, and out of our line of sight before we jumped back in the car and sped off back to the party we were missing for this little escapade.

It was only upon my return when I found a group huddled around Chara, trying to console her, that I came to realize she'd thought Jerry was going for the final ride of his life. We all had a good laugh and soon forgot about Jerry or the suspected plot of his demise. The nickname, however, was not forgotten, at least by Jimbo. I'm not sure that he even remembers my real name. I have been Danger to him ever since.

I must have been seventeen when I outran my first police officer. It was two in the morning, and I was delivering some product when I saw him at a four way stop sign coming in the opposite direction. I couldn't imagine why he would've wanted to pull me over, a teenager out at that time on a Tuesday, but he hit his lights when he saw me come to a stop. I instantly floored it, and by the time he spun his cruiser around I was gone. I recall seeing only red and blue lights reflected on the treetops in my rearview mirror, I was that far ahead of him.

Soon after, Eddie went back to prison on a parole violation, and I had to move our lab and enough chemicals to produce several kilos of the drug. I loaded up my Camero and headed out to meet up with a trusted friend who owned a secluded plot of land deep in the woods.

It was most likely because of that prior incident that, while I was transporting the lab, I passed a cop going in the opposite direction and he flipped a U-turn to what I assume was to pull me over. I never gave him the chance; I floored it and took off like a shot.

Again, I never saw the front of his vehicle once I hit the gas. *This is getting too easy,* I thought at the time.

Now, I'm not one to blame my bad behavior on the media or television warping my sense of values. However, I did justify my actions, at least in my head, by comparing myself to the Duke boys. They were just good ol' boys trying to outrun Rosco while smuggling a still to a safer location. The only difference I saw was that I drove a Chevy and I was smuggling a meth lab.

My young, drug-addled brain did not compute the obvious nature of my situation. I lived in Paradise, California, a town of about 25,000 people at that time. There were probably twenty cops on the force, and I must have stood out like a sore thumb. There weren't many 1977 sky blue Camaros running around town being driven by a long-haired teenager at that time. How many? Turns out, just one.

I pulled into town after five days of laying low at my new partner's place in the woods, and wouldn't you know it, I was pulled over before getting a mile past the town limits.

I had taken care to devoid myself and my car of any drug paraphernalia beforehand. However, they did find my pistol which had been in my trunk and inside a case with a padlock. Nothing illegal about that. That is, unless the cops write it up as possession of a loaded firearm. I never kept the gun loaded, but because there was a clip in the case alongside the pistol, they wrote up the booking sheet as "loaded."

I never admitted it had been me that had outrun the police on either occasion, but nevertheless I was booked on the gun and reckless driving charges. Driving at speeds over 100mph. The cop told me he despised me for my crime, but did compliment me on my driving skills, navigating the twists and turns of the road we were on at such high speeds. I was released on my own recognizance that time (no bail required) with an order to appear in court.

The police had their eyes on me after that, and it wasn't long before they caught me in a routine traffic stop for supposedly not using a turn signal. They found over two ounces of product and several thousand dollars in cash on me that day. This time I was taken to jail for the first time. I was booked on possession, possession for sale, and transporting narcotics.

When the police report came out it said that I had only had eight grams of meth and a few hundred dollars on me at the time of my arrest. I was not so shocked at the missing money, but the drugs perplexed me. Shouldn't the cops have wanted to nail me with as much product as possible to earn me a stiffer sentence? And just what did they do with it? Were they meth heads too? My attorney just said, "Welcome to the justice system."

I spent all the money I had amassed on attorney fees and court fines to eventually be sentenced to simple possession. I received a three-year suspended sentence and was sent on my way.

I tried to live a somewhat normal life after that, no longer pursuing the life of a meth cook. Oh, I didn't stop using it. In fact, I got busted again either for a dirty urine test or simple possession, I don't recall which, and I had to do six months in the county jail for violating my probation.

I guess my attorney felt he'd made enough money off me the first time and he took pity on me now that I was broke, and he convinced the judge not to impose the suspended three-year sentence he could have. All for no charge.

After my release I began a relationship with a woman who had two daughters—a nine-year-old and a baby. I loved those kids as if they were my own, and we eventually added another daughter to the brood.

No matter how much I loved them and wanted to be a good dad, the drug always came first. It came before paying the rent, the utilities and sometimes even food. It was a constant source of tension in the relationship.

I got and lost jobs in every sector where you could get hired without having to pass a drug test. Restaurants, construction, floor covering, and tile work, to name a few.

There were some good stretches of time when we were making the bills and life seemed to be going well, but without fail I would screw it up.

I had a friend who for years tried to get me a job where he worked at a tree service company. It was a coveted job in our area that paid good money and offered excellent benefits. He could get me in if I could just pass a drug test. It only takes seventy-two hours for meth to be out of your system, but I couldn't do it.

"Dude, just stop long enough to pass the test. They don't test you after you're hired," he pleaded with me, but I could never do it.

The relationship with my daughter's mom ended, and I hooked up with the craziest woman I'd ever met. I quickly learned that she was not just bipolar and a full-blown alcoholic but was a junkie as well. Funny how my high and mighty morals so quickly took a back seat when it came to someone I was sexually involved with.

She seemed to make it her life's mission to bring me into the fold of intravenous users of the drug. First, she revealed to me that some of the people we knew who I'd always considered to have their shit together, were in fact using needles. I couldn't believe it; it shattered my long-held beliefs about it.

These were people who maintained pleasant homes, took care of their kids, and weren't known for any of the scandalous things I'd always associated with junkies.

My girlfriend would also make little remarks about the bulging veins in my arms, especially if I'd just been doing some sort of manual labor.

"Damn, look at those veins in your forearms! I could hit that so easy." It was like living with a vampire!

Another approach she took was to tell me how little of the drug was needed to get high with. This was intriguing to me because we could afford so little of it at the time.

She eventually won me over and I caved in. The things that the drug had slowly been taking from me over the years immediately accelerated, and I began a downward spiral that was utterly beyond my control. Every last shred of morality and decency was gone before long. I had become what I had despised so vehemently at the beginning of my dance with this drug. A junkie!

Soon I was stealing everything, from lawn mowers and yard equipment from people's lawns in the dark of night, to food and alcohol from local grocery stores.

I was lying to my family and friends to get money from them, and even stealing from them if I couldn't convince them to help me.

The allure meth was too powerful, and I got back into manufacturing the drug again, but it was never enough. No amount crank could fill the void that it had eaten away inside of me. I could not save myself. I needed to be rescued. Thankfully, law enforcement was there to do just that.

I was arrested on a burglary charge and began an education that would forever shape the way I lead my life.

Chapter Four

WE AIN'T IN KANSAS NO MORE

2:30 AM, COUNTY JAIL, 1997. "Gilford, roll it up!" came the announcement over the intercom of my two-man cell. My heart raced even though I knew nothing exciting would be happening for hours to come. I slid down off my top bunk and gathered my meager possessions. A note pad, about fifty stamped envelopes to be used for cash when we reached the prison, and my bed roll. I heard the buzz, and then the clank of my cell door unlocking, and I pushed my way out the door, bed roll under one arm, and paperwork under the other. It was graduation day. I'd spent my time in the bush leagues; I was being called up to the Majors.

They marched me down to the booking cage with about twelve other dudes from various cells and dorms throughout the jail. Some of these guys had already been in prison and had to come back to county jail to face additional charges before being shipped back where they had been. A few of us were first timers to the big house and we stood out like a sore thumb. Then there were some who had been to the joint before but were headed back on fresh charges.

We newbies were the ones asking all the questions, looking bright eyed and nervous; the old timers were just trying to take a nap. While we waited for the bus to come for us, the deputies brought out two more inmates for transport: green jumpsuit guys. Now in my county jail, the color of your jump suit said a lot about you. Yellow jumpsuits meant you had some serious mental issues, like suicide-watch-kind-of-serious. Orange meant you were one of the masses, just a regular bloke, in for everyday shit. Red meant you were exceptionally dangerous, in for murder or rape or maybe both. Green was PC or protective custody. This meant that you had to be kept separate from the rest of the inmates because you'd be beaten, raped, or killed for some reason or another. The two usual reasons were that they were child molesters, or they were rats. Either way, the bottom of the barrel. These guys, they locked up in a separate room away from the rest of us while we waited.

After long hours of sitting on a concrete floor, the prison bus finally arrived, and they began cuffing us—both wrists and ankles—prior to shuffling us out the door and onto the bus. The green jumpsuit guys were brought out last and they had their own individual seats on the bus with walls of heavy metal mesh surrounding them to keep them safe from the rest of us.

I don't do well on bus rides or any vehicle where I'm not in the front seat. Motion sickness hits me fast, and this was no exception. Thankfully, the bus stopped at just about every county jail along the way which gave my stomach time to settle. Barfing is never fun, but doing so with cuffed hands and feet would've really sucked.

Eventually we arrived at our destination, a hell hole in central California, all made of bricks, steel, and razor wire. The level of security at this place made county jail's look like the velvet rope used to block people from entering a nightclub. There was multiple razor-wired gates we had to pass through, each one requiring an inspection of the bus inside and out, over the top and underneath. The guards had big mirrors on long poles they'd use to check the top and underside of the bus—basically selfie sticks twenty years before their invention. Once we reached the entrance, a screw from the joint climbed onto the bus to bark some commands at us. "Listen up! When you exit this vehicle, you will move to your right and keep moving until you are instructed to stop." Memories of the movie Stripes flashed through my head. We did as we were instructed and moved down the aisle to the exit with our ankle chains restricting our steps to no more than a few inches at a time. When we got to the steps leading off the bus we were faced with another challenge, the steps were too tall for the length of our chains, so we had to hop. We couldn't use the handrail either because our wrists were cuffed to a chain around our waist. Thankfully, when I lost my balance the guy in front of me was close enough to impede my fall. At the county jail, the deputy sheriffs helped us on board, but here we were left to our own devices.

Once we were all lined up beside the bus, I was surprised to see the PC boys standing next to us. No segregation for them from here on out, it appeared.

They herded us inside the building and had us line up against a wall once again. Here we had to strip down completely naked, after our shackles were removed of course. Then they took us three at a time a little further down the wall to stand in front of waiting officers who would conduct a thorough body search. I was in the middle of the line, so I got to see this scene play out a few times before it was my turn. This gave me a chance to know what to expect so as to not screw up and draw the ire of the guards.

The CO's inspected every inch of our naked bodies for contraband with practiced instructions, "Raise your arms. Run your fingers through your hair. Open your mouth and lift your tongue. Let me see behind your ears. Lift your belly fat. Pull back your foreskin. Turn around and face the wall. Let me see the bottoms of your feet. Bend over, squat and cough while spreading your butt cheeks. Next."

When my turn came, I wound up in front of the scariest looking CO I had seen yet. A six-foot-four-inch-tall Black man with muscles bulging from under his uniform. He wore black sunglasses and a scowl. The sunglasses seemed absurd in the dark corridor, but I wasn't going to tell him so. I had the routine down from watching the guys who went before me, so I started to raise my arms, but he threw me for a loop by asking me to open my mouth first. "Get your damn arms down, nobody told you to raise your arms, boy! He shouted at me. Looking back, I'm sure that this little ploy was something they would do for amusement. Let the guys get see the same orders person after person, then switch it up when a newbie-looking sucker came along.

When it came time for me to bend over, spread my cheeks and cough, I got yelled at again. "I said spread 'em! I can't see!" I performed the demeaning act again, and again I was yelled at. "I said I can't see!" *Take off your fucking sunglasses,* I thought, but bent over even further until I almost toppled over. Finally, it was enough, and I heard him bark, "Next!"

Eventually we had all been inspected and humiliated enough. They crowded us into a small room where they dumped a big bag of wrinkly jumpsuits in the middle of the floor for us to scavenge through. I assume the ones we wore to the prison were being sent back to the county jails. In the end, nobody wound up with a jumpsuit that fit, but we were told we would get a clothing issue in a few days. My pant legs were about twelve inches too long, so I just had to cuff the bottoms. Other guys had suits that wouldn't zip over their belly's girth, had broken zippers, or were so tight they'd be singing soprano.

From there we were taken into a room with benches along all four walls. We each found a place and stared blankly at each other from across the room. A military looking man in a sergeant's uniform entered the room, salt and pepper hair fashioned in a crew cut, barrel chest, and arms like tree trunks. "Gentlemen," he began in a booming voice that matched his looks, "welcome to state prison. Let me start off by saying you are not in county jail anymore. Forget everything you knew about the rules in county jail, we do things different here at the state level. The sheriff at the county jail doesn't want his deputies putting their hands on the inmates, here we encourage it. If you step out of line or give one of my officers any flack, you can expect a beating like you've never known before. When you're on the yard and you look up and see the guard towers, those men and women in those towers are armed with rifles with actual bullets in them. Should the alarm sound, you are to drop where you are, flat on your belly. Don't run for cover or try to find a soft piece of earth to drop on. Any movement they see when the alarm is sounding will be seen as an act of aggression or attempted escape and they will act accordingly." The guy sitting next to me leaned over and whispered in my ear, "Guess we ain't in Kansas no more." The sergeant spun to face the Whisperer, "Officer Reynolds, please escort this gentleman to the SHU," he said matter of factly. One of the screws who were scattered about the room strode over to him and latched his hands onto Whisperer's wrist and shoulder, and in a well-practiced maneuver, pulled him off the bench and onto the ground. Reynolds landed with his full body weight in the center of his culprits back as he twisted his arms behind his back to receive the cuffs. He used Whisperer's head as support when he rose. He then pulled the poor bastard up by the hand cuffs in what seemed to be a painful wrenching of his limbs. He was hustled out of the room and presumably off to the Special Housing Unit.

"Gentlemen," the Sergeant continued, "any contrary behavior such as this will be met with immediate action. As the man said, you ain't in Kansas no more."

"Speaking of the SHU, any of you folks who came from protective custody, and now find yourselves in the mix with the general population, don't fret, you have the opportunity to make a fresh start. You can choose now to remain in general population or opt to spend your entire sentence in the SHU. Our special housing unit is unlike the segregated living you were experiencing in county jail. In the SHU you'll be in complete isolation. You will not go to the yard. Three times a week you will have an hour of sunlight exposure in another isolated cage. So, think long and hard about opting for this choice. On the other hand, if you feel that you are truly in danger, this may be right for you" It was after that statement that one of our previously green-jumpsuit-clad fellows raised his hand and asked to be placed in the SHU. We all instinctively looked to the other PC who looked about nervously but remained silent. An officer took the one guy away in cuffs, but in a much more civil manner than the Whisperer's treatment.

There was a lot more from the Sergeant on how we should conduct ourselves on the inside, laden with threats of the consequences should we not adopt his advice.

Eventually the orientation ended, and we were brought outside to an enclosed area about forty feet squared. A chain link fence separated us from the general population. The experienced guys made a beeline for the fences where they could converse with dudes on the other side. The wheeling and dealing commenced as I saw stamped envelopes going through the fence and tobacco coming back through. We'd all spent a long time in county jail without the comfort of tobacco, and it was clearly a first priority on all our minds. There was a steep markup for buying just inside the prison. A bag of Bugler tobacco sold for about a buck back then on the commissary, and a stamped envelope cost about 25 cents. The going rate for a pack of Bugler at the fence exchange was going for twenty stamped envelopes, and we were all happy to pay it. Economics 101: supply and demand.

The supply of tobacco ran out before I could make my score, but there were a few guys kind enough to let me bum a smoke off of them.

Once the fevered trading had ceased and I was enjoying my first smoke in three months, I noticed a group of guys chatting with some hard-ass looking dudes on the other side of the fence. It was clear from their body language that they were pointing out the lone guy left from our PC arrivals. PC Guy was clearly aware he was the topic of discussion as well; he was fidgeting nervously alone in his own corner of the enclosure.

Eventually the screws began coming for us in groups of two or three to take us to our next places of residences. I was called to the gate with along with PC Guy, and we followed our jailors down endless corridors and through many locked gates until we reached our cell block. There they relayed our names to the CO's in charge of the block and they in turn gave us directions to our cells. We walked twenty-five yards across the concrete floor, past stainless-steel tables and chairs that were spread out between the rows of cells that lined each of the walls. Halfway down the cell block we parted ways. He climbed the stairs on one side, while I climbed the stairs on the other. We both were on the third floor, directly across from one another. I was relieved to find when I arrived at my cell, a pleasant enough looking guy awaiting my arrival behind the bars. My door slid open, and I heard, "Inmate, enter!" from a CO downstairs. My cell door slid open with all the subtlety of a freight train crashing down the tracks. I stepped inside as the door slammed close behind me. I got a friendly "hey" from my new celly just before we heard a ruckus from across the way. We both crowded to the bars of the door to investigate the commotion. We had a clear view into the cell that PC Guy had entered. The sound of fists hitting flesh and bone was unmistakable even if we hadn't been able to see the pummeling, he was receiving from his new celly. It was a blur of limbs flying from where we stood, but I could see enough to know that PC Guy was not faring well. The sound of boots stomping up metal stairs soon joined the cacophony of the beating as members of the goon squad charged up to the third floor.

The whole thing lasted no more than a minute or two but judging from the bloody and battered face of PC Guy as he was removed from the cell, it must have felt like a lifetime for him. Surprisingly, his cell mate who'd delivered the beating seemed to be treated in a much more dignified manner as the two were removed from the cell and ushered away. PC Guy was shoved and pushed all the way down the gangplank and down the stairs, while his attacker was calmly placed in handcuffs and escorted slowly down the same path. The CO's even held his arms as he navigated the stairs, making sure that if he lost his footing he wouldn't fall.

It was instantly apparent that news of PC Guy's history had reached his would-be celly, and he had acted appropriately. Amazing. How could he have gotten that news so fast? How would those inmates from the yard know PC Guys destination? Finally, were the screws in on it? Because they certainly seemed to be less sympathetic to the guy who'd been beaten, than to the one who did the beating!

I turned to my new celly who kindly said, "You won't get any of that here."

This clearly this wasn't Kansas anymore, and it was quite a shock to see so much violence on my first day in the joint. I had started a journal back in county jail, and wrote my reflections down that evening as I lay upon my bunk. I noted I needed to be on guard now more than ever. I was a wise cracking guy by nature, and Whisperer's comments were exactly the sort I'd normally make.

The level of power these guards had over me was also apparent. In county, although my freedom was taken from me, I never feared the guards. Quite the opposite. I saw them as being there to protect us should anything go down. Here, I now knew, I would have to show these men and women the utmost respect. They were not playing!

Thirdly the principles of economy were alive and well, even in prison. I knew I'd have to make wise choices about my purchases, regardless of my desires. It was good that I couldn't get any tobacco at the fence line just inside the prison; I would have gone broke before I ever had the chance to get to the commissary.

The yard commerce reminded me of my dad. He was always big on the latest technology. I recall he paid nearly one thousand dollars for a VCR and receiver set when they first came on to the market. One year later, you could buy one for about one hundred dollars, and I think the last one I ever purchased cost me about twenty bucks. Clearly instant gratification is sweet, but patience is often the wiser choice.

The last part of my entry that night was on choices. My choices landed me in prison, so I'd better make it work for me in the long run. Sometimes the least attractive choice can end up being the best. PC Guy took a chance and opted to stay in general population, and it cost him dearly. I've had to make unsavory choices since then in my life and have been better for them. Whether it was the decision to end an unhappy marriage, which later gave me the opportunity to meet my true soulmate or leaving a job which I felt lacked future promise to take one where I had to start back at the entry level in order to have a better long-term possibility of growth.

I had never been able to make the best choices for my life while in the grips of addiction. The immediate needs and desires always outweighed those of the long term. A five-year plan? I couldn't look past the next five hours, let alone five days!

My first day in prison showed me that I had a lot to learn. Thankfully I had plenty of time to figure it out as I embarked on this journey to not only survive life in the joint, but to remake myself into the kind of man I wanted to be.

Chapter Five

CHOOSE YOUR WORDS CAREFULLY

IT ONLY TOOK A few weeks to realize this place was a real shithole. We're talking Shawshank redemption! It was dark and damp, and just as depressing a scene as one could imagine. The cots were metal frames with some sort of woven springs that supported what had once been mattresses but were now no more than remnants of stuffing that you had to contain inside a sheet with its corners tied together.

I had been moved to a six-man cell while awaiting the fate that would decide which prison would be my destination. This was merely a reception and designation center, a weigh station if you will. They gave us psych evaluations, checked us for diseases and parasites, evaluated what level of prison security we merited, asked about any gang affiliations, and tried to determine if we had any known enemies in the system in their quest to place us in the most appropriate location.

To say I was on high alert would be an understatement. I'm sure I stood out as a newbie to the veterans I shared that cell with. I was searching my memory constantly for the tips and rules of prison life I'd learned along the way, on the lookout for potential threats that would label me a bitch, or in any way compromise my standing in prison society. The class system was pretty straightforward; murder, bank robbery with a gun, smuggling, manufacturing methamphetamine, these types of convictions were top tier. Possession of drugs, selling drugs, theft, bank robbery by handing the teller a note, these were more middle tier. Rats, punks, rapists, and child molesters were the bottom of the barrel. Being too scared to fight or getting pushed around landed you closer to the bottom no matter what you were in for.

I was in the middle tier and had no intention of sliding down. I was sitting on the edge of my bunk with my feet on the floor trying to read a book, but really just looking at the same few lines over and over again. All my concentration was on guys moving about the cell to use the toilet/sink combo placed at the end of the cell, or just having conversations around me was taking all of my concentration.

One guy walked up near the foot of my bunk and started chatting with the guy in the next one over. My Spidey-senses tingled as I prepared for trouble. He stood there talking with the guy who lay on his bunk, chatting about nothing in particular for a few minutes. Then the guy who lay in the bunk sat up, and my guy sat on the foot of my bed to better face his pal. In my mind, this was it, I either asserted myself or faced the consequences. "Dude, don't sit on my bed, man." I deepened my voice for effect. He only turned his head slightly in my direction and said "Yeah, just a minute man," before turning his attention back to his pal. This was it alright, I had to make the right move, or I was fucked. I considered my next move.

Do I start swinging? Do I scream to let him know I mean business? I decided to play it cool and give him another chance. This time I tapped him on the shoulder and in a calm, but firm voice said, "I'm serious man, you can't be sitting on my bunk." Again, he only turned his head slightly, paused, then replied, "Just give me a second man." My blood boiled, I felt a cold sweat flood my lower back and arm pits, and I choked back my rage as I poked him firmly in the shoulder and raised my voice a few decibels, "Get off my bunk *now!*" This time I'd gotten his attention. He turned to look at me and simply asked, "Or what?" I began in measured tones, "You get off my bunk," I stood to tower over him, "or *I'll BEAT YOU OFF!*" I immediately regretted the phrasing! There was a long pause of silence in the cell as I felt all attention turning towards us. The cold sweat turned into a deluge, dripping down the crack of my ass. My face burned hot with fear and embarrassment, and I smelled the stench of my body odor wafting into my nostrils. Somewhere behind me the silence was broken by a guy affecting a feminine voice, "Oh, sign me up!" Another guy from behind me chimed in, "Me too!" I could hear the feet move across the floor as the men started to file in behind me. "Line starts here fellas," another girly voice rang out. *Fuck!*

I stood there with my fists balled, looking down at the source of my current predicament. He had his head down, slowly shaking it back and forth and slightly convulsing in what I thought was building anger. When he looked up, I could see that he was trying to restrain his laughter. He raised his hands, palms out, in a gesture of surrender and he rose from my cot. "Okay kid, I get what you're trying to do, but you gotta choose your words carefully." He took me under his arm and walked me to a corner of the cell as everyone else went back to doing whatever they'd been up to before the excitement had started.

We had a nice long chat which gave me time to cool down and gather my wits again. He gave me some good advice like: Watch a person's body language to know if they're truly being hostile, and don't be so quick to escalate a situation. If you find yourself actually being punked, then you act. Lastly, he told me, "Never send anyone a post-card." By which he meant not to give a head's up by threatening someone. If you need to start swinging, just do it.

That evening's journal entry began with "choose your words carefully." That along with being able to read the room objectively, were skills I needed to work on. Clearly, he'd been in the wrong for not asking permission to sit upon my bunk, but he hadn't been trying to "punk me out," he was just absentminded in his actions while chatting with a pal.

Chapter Six

IF YOU NO HAVE MONEY FOR FRAJOS, YOU NO SMOKE FRAJOS

I DON'T RECALL HOW I came to be Billy Goat's pinochle partner, but I do recall everything about him. He was a grizzled-looking old dude with a salt and pepper head of hair and a long Van Dyke that matched. A first name of Bill and that facial hair was all he needed to earn himself the nickname "Billy Goat." We won a lot of games which brought us many challengers who wanted to take down the old man and the kid. I'm fairly sure Billy kept me on as a partner not because he was able to make up for my shortcomings, but more likely because I made him laugh. Whenever I'd win a trick or make a great play, I'd follow it up with something like, "Now that's puttin' some stank on it!" Or "Don't put your kids in the street if you don't want them getting run over!" I'd also slip into different accents for no other reason than to entertain Billy and myself, like my Scottish one that he was particularly fond of, "Aye ya laddy, yoor not genna tek meh withoot a right proper fight, ya dirty cunt!"

We didn't get to go out to the yard very often, but they would unlock our cells pretty much every day for an hour or two. That would give us a chance play cards at one of the tables that ran down the center of the block on the first floor. There were probably a dozen tables for six hundred inmates stacked two to a cell, three stories high, so getting a table was a luxury. Luckily for us, Billy Goat's cell was located on the first floor, so he always got us a table. The only trouble with the table was its close proximity to the wall of telephones located just a few steps away.

Inmates were allowed to make collect calls at an exorbitant rate to those who accepted the charges. I rarely called home to Mom for this reason, but also because doing time was a lot easier for me if I blocked out all thoughts of home, and just stuck to my daily routine. "Sticking to your program," they called it on the inside. Though I would call at least once a month to assure my mother that her little boy was okay, and that I loved her.

Billy Goat always took the seat with his back to the telephones. That way he could keep an eye on the majority of the population. I had a more limited view, but I saw plenty from my position directly across from him. For example, the guy in the cell on the second floor above where Billy sat was running a tattoo studio. I could see his clients entering, quickly followed by the faint buzz of the tattoo gun made from a portable cassette player and other scavenged materials. A lookout would always be posted just outside the entrance to his cell, pretending to be enjoying the lone ray of sunlight that filtered its way through bars and windows from the outside.

One floor up from the tattoo parlor and a little further down was where Chewy resided. Chewy was the drug dealer. He had a steady stream of visitors, and he too had the obligatory lookouts posted on either side of his cell door trying to look inconspicuous. Chewy was a purveyor of all kinds of products, but heroin was the real cash cow. After all, you didn't want to be locked up on a drug that intensifies your reality. Better to be on one that dulls the senses so you could escape your reality. I myself was playing it straight. The embarrassment and shame of not only how I'd been living my life, but of the pain I had caused my mother was something I was determined not to repeat. I had to completely rehabilitate myself, and doing the things I had always done was not going to bring me different results.

About halfway down the second-floor tier on the edge of my peripheral view was the punk palace. This is where our two homosexual inhabitants had their cell. Any openly gay man in the joint was referred to as a punk, and these two inmates happened to be transgender as well. They had both been taking hormones to develop breasts, which made them immensely popular to those who were willing to pay for their services. If a punk thought a person was cute, they would often shower their crush with gifts of cigarettes or drugs in an effort to get what they wanted. I was fine being abstinent. Normally Blacks and Whites are not paired together in a cell, punks represented their own segment of the complex code of unwritten prison dynamics. Case in point; Blacks and Whites couldn't share a meal together, but punks can only share meals which each other, negating the Black/White rule. No one of any race could share a meal with a punk, yet it was perfectly fine to visit a punk for sexual favors, as long as the punk was of your race, and you didn't break bread together. I don't condone the rules of prison life, by the way, but this is the system in which I found myself.

All this I learned through casual glances and bits of conversations I had at the pinochle table. It was not cool, and quite dangerous actually, to be caught staring at someone, especially those engaged in rule-breaking activity. We never had full blown conversations about any of this either, just comments made here and there that helped to paint a pretty clear picture of the events that were unfolding on our cell block. Things like, "I see Tim's getting some dust knocked off of it at the punk palace," or "Johnny's slinging a lot of ink up there today."

Billy Goat and I had been playing cards with a couple of older Mexican guys, Toro, and Shadow. It was acceptable to play cards with another race as long as you weren't gambling. Sort of neutral ground, I suppose. Gambling could lead to arguing, and arguing could lead to fighting, and if a fight broke out between two or more guys of differing races it could escalate to an all-out riot. We actually did gamble, but only for pushups. The losers had to do one pushup for every point they had lost by. Thankfully, we rarely lost (thanks to my partner) because I was seriously overweight and out of shape at this point in my life, so doing any more than 10 pushups had to be done in installments!

Shadow was a classic Chicano: jet black hair that he wore slicked straight back. He had an enormous black mustache that looked like a push broom along with a soul patch below his bottom lip. Prisoners could check out an iron by leaving their ID card with the guard at the cage, and clearly Shadow was skilled in the art of ironing. He wore his pressed blue shirt buttoned only at the collar, and his pants were belted high on his waist with crisp pleats running down the front of each leg. He had the frame on an NFL linebacker, but he was a quiet guy. He had a dry sense of humor that made playing cards with him fun. "Oh no, pappi," he'd say when a round of cards was turning in our favor. Toro could have been an actor in one of those telenovelas that played on the Spanish channel. Dark hair parted with razor precision to one side and a pencil thin mustache groomed meticulously perched upon his upper lip. Toro was profoundly serious about his card playing, and you could tell that his every play was calculated as he processed all the possibilities of the game. He rarely spoke, except when to bid his hand, or to berate Shadow after a poor play. He'd do this in Spanish, his temple vein bulging out while he did so. Toro was a thin and short man, but I would not have wanted to tangle with him. He must have been in his fifties, but I could tell by the lean muscles that were well defined beneath his brown forearms and the chiseled line of his jaw that he would be a formidable foe.

It was at this table with the aforementioned players that I first became aware of a fellow we would eventually come to nickname, "Bed Head." I heard him before I saw him. He was on the phone just on the edge of my vision. "Babe, I'm hurting in here. Can you just please figure out a way to send me my care package?" he was pleading in hushed and pathetic tones to what I assumed was his wife or girlfriend. The care package he was referring to was a box of goods you could have sent in once every three months. It could weigh up to thirty pounds and have all kinds of items from a pre-approved list like sneakers, cigarettes, cans of meat, and toiletries. Once your package arrived at the prison, you'd be called down to receiving and discharge (R&D), where an officer would open the box and go through its contents. He would pull out items that were not allowed, and generally make sure there was no contraband hiding in any of the products.

Now I'd heard dozens of guys making this request on the phones before, but this was the first where I thought the guy was on the verge of tears while doing so. His voice was quivering, and he was sniffing in quick gusts of air like a toddler who'd just had a toy taken from him. I glanced over to take a peek at this miserable wretch and saw a hot mess leaning on his forearm which was perched across the top of the pay phone. He had a giant mop of ginger colored curly hair that looked like it could be harboring a pack of squirrels. Half of his shirt was untucked, but the other half was tucked into his tighty-whitey briefs which were riding up a good three inches above the waistline of his trousers. Speaking of his waistline, it was girthy to say the least. His five-foot-five frame must have been supporting a good two hundred and seventy pounds of gelatinous, fleshy rolls.

I turned from this scene and exchanged raised eyebrows with my fellow card players. "Anyone got a smoke I can bum?" I asked the table.

"You have any dinero?" Toro asked.

"No, but I'll pay you back when I get my commissary."

"I'll tell you something my papa used to tell me, and it's a very good lesson for life mijo. You no have money for frajos, you no smoke the frajos."

It didn't seem like a very profound lesson in life at the time,
Just a snarky way of not lending anyone a smoke.

I heard Bed Head finishing up his conversation, "Oh thank you so much, baby, thank you! Yeah, yeah, I know, but you'll try, right? Oh, thank you! Yes, I will. I love you too!" There was a pep in his step as I watched him make a beeline up to Chewy's cell. He paused long enough to have an animated discussion with one of the henchmen posted outside the cell before being admitted in. I looked over at Toro who had also been following this chain of events, and he repeated his sage advice, "You no have dineros for frajos, you no smoke the frajos."

It was a few minutes later that Bead Head emerged looking calm and heavy lidded. He rubbed his face a few times, scratched his upper arms and chest before shuffling his way back to his own cell with a dreamy, happy look upon his chubby face.   Bed Head made daily trips back to Chewy's cell for the next week or so. Eventually, though, he had some trouble making it past the henchmen into Chewy's cell. It was clear that he had to do some persuading, whereas before he had basically been strolling in with no more than a nod to those posted outside the cell. Soon he was back on the phone, "Dammit babe, where's my package? What? No, I paid that, I swear! No, I didn't keep the receipt! You're out there with the world at your fingertips, and I'm wasting away in here!" His phone calls went generally along those lines for the next few days. I was able to surmise from the bits I overheard that he'd left his family in dire financial straits, and yet somehow believed that his wife was living high on the hog out there trying to support herself and their kids on a single income with all their bills in arrears, thanks to him.

He was no longer being granted entrance to Chewy's cell, and he'd even stopped trying. In fact, now the henchmen were making visits to Bed Head's cell on a daily basis. Each time he'd been paid a visit, he would immediately march over to the phone banks, and resume his pleas and demands for his package. He was in the throes of withdrawal, and he looked it. His pale and pasty skin had taken on a greenish hue.

As he walked away from the phone dejected one day, Billy Goat's eyes followed his path as he shuffled away. "Won't be long now. Surprised Chewy let it go on this long," Billy whispered with a touch of sorrow in his voice. I knew something bad was coming for Bed Head, I just didn't know what. I felt bad for the guy, for no good reason. I mean he totally brought this on himself, and he was nothing but a self-centered asshole where his family was concerned. Yet you knew the consequences would be severe. The fact that he hadn't checked himself into the SHU boggled the mind. It was especially hard to watch because it brought me back to what I had been like when I was back on the streets, begging and pleading with people just to get my fix. Rarely a day goes by that I don't have a flash of memories of some horrible thing I did or said in the interest of obtaining my drug.

Then, one day a miracle happened: a page came over the loudspeaker, "Inmate Leary, report to R&D to pick up your care package." You would've thought he'd just hit the lottery! All signs of his being in heavy withdrawal from heroin vanished. He came bursting out of his cell pumping his arms in the air like Rocky at the top of the steps in Philadelphia. "Yeah baby!" He exclaimed. He strode towards the guard cage to wait to be released at the next gate unlock when he would be allowed to make his way to R&D. His walk was animated, reminiscent of the classic George Jefferson strut. He gave a grin and a nod up to a henchman outside Chewy's cell. The henchman shook his head and walked away, clearly not happy with the attention Bed Head was drawing.

The boys and I continued our card game until lockdown, which they always did about an hour before dinner. We were all tucked away in our cells when the workers began returning from their jobs all over the compound, including my celly Tim, who worked in R&D. "Welcome home celly," I greeted him in the usual fashion. "Fun day at work?"

"Yes actually, today *was* rather fun. Bed Head got his package."

"No kidding? I saw him heading out to get it in a rather jovial mood, but I didn't see him return."

"He came back with us, and he isn't in a jovial mood any longer." I simply raised an eyebrow. "It was dog food," he told me as he kicked off his prison issued boots and slipped into his plastic sandals that doubled as slippers and shower shoes.

"Oh, you mean it was junk food, like that Dinty Moore stew shit. I hate that garbage!"

"No man, it was a giant sack of dog food! His old lady had written all over it in black marker. It said, 'here's your package, you fucking dog! I know about your whore, the money, everything!' CO Davis did all he could not to laugh in his face while he was telling him that dog food was not on the approved list of acceptable items."

Bed Head stayed in his cell when we were released for chow hall that night, and again the next morning for breakfast. The boys and I were back at the pinochle table later that morning when I noticed Chewy and his henchmen conversing while they looked down into Bed Head's cell. Discussing his fate, no doubt.

We were about two games into the day when I witnessed three henchmen traveling down the stairs from Chewy's. They made a stop at another cell along their route and picked up another two henchmen, subcontractors it would seem. Then the five of them made their way to Bed Head's cell and crowded in. A moment later Bed Head's celly came walking out buttoning his shirt as he left. His hair was messy, and he was misaligning the buttonholes in his shirt as he made his way from the cell. He must have been taking a nap when he'd been invited to leave. The sounds of fists hitting flesh followed immediately upon the celly's departure. I averted my gaze and tried to concentrate on my cards. "And so, it begins," Billy Goat whispered. "Let's hope a beating is all he gets."

The beating lasted several minutes before it seemed to descend into what sounded like wrestling. Bed Head's cell was just out of my line of sight, and I had to force myself not to turn my head to look. Too many heads turned in their direction could get the guards' attention, and you didn't want to be the cause of that! The sounds, however, traveled quite clearly to our ears at the table, and it was soon obvious that the beating was just the beginning. Next came the sounds of flesh slapping flesh and muffled screams and heavy breathing. Bed Head was getting raped! Toro leaned over to me and held my gaze, "Papi, you no have money for frajos, you no smoke frajos."

This scene played out for two more days before Bed Head had enough and checked himself into the SHU. I think once would have done it for me, but he was clearly an optimist.

I reflected that night on Toro's "you no have money for frajos, you no smoke frajos." It seemed like just a catchy thing to say, but in retrospect it proved to be quite profound indeed.

Though my creditors would never attack or rape me, I do get a little anxiety whenever I'm about to go into debt of any kind. The first time I financed a used car, for instance. I can still feel the tightness in my chest I felt that day at the dealership. Buying a home for the first time was surprisingly less stressful. Probably because I wasn't doing it alone, and the house itself was collateral for the loan.

I also thought and wrote about loyalty to those who love me. Bed Head's woman was most definitely in a state of financial crisis. Suddenly she had been thrust into a position of having to care for their small children all on her own, plus trying to support her man in prison. From all appearances she was trying to get Bed Head his package at what would have been a great hardship for her and the kids, but when his lies and secrets came to light, she focused all her energy into sending him a message. Loved ones are your best allies in life—don't fuck it up.

I think the hardest thing I had to admit was the similarities between Bed Head and myself. Sometimes the only way to see your own ugly behavior is to see it in someone else. Bed Head had been a hideous reflection of the person I had been just a few months earlier, and it hurt to accept that reality.

Chapter Seven
FINDING JESUS

Finding Jesus in prison is a cliché, I get it, but that's just what I did. Trust me, I was first to make fun of people for this very thing. However, when you find yourself at a crossroads like I did—a life in shambles, addicted to drugs and having lost every last shred of dignity and self-respect—you have some tough choices to make. So, I, like a lot of people, decided I needed to change not just some things in my life, but everything in my life. Mind, body, and spirit.

It all started with reading the Bible. The *whole* Bible. I had always avoided learning about God because I felt it would stop all the fun I was having. I had this crazy notion that if I didn't know specifically what God didn't want me to be doing, then I wouldn't be punished for not knowing in the afterlife. Of course, I had heard the of ten commandments before, but I hadn't actually read them. Besides, wasn't there a "new deal" in the New Testament? Surely that new deal was a much more lenient one.

So, there I was at the lowest point in my life: Facing years in prison, and all the illusions of my being a regular Joe who just happened to use meth like some people drank beer, was over.

I was still in county jail awaiting trial when I first picked up a Bible. I lay on my bunk and started reading from page one. The only time I'd ever read any books was during my meth-fueled high school studies, so beginning this mighty tome clean and sober was daunting to say the least. I figured I had plenty of time on my hands, so why not?

As the days and weeks passed, I read my way through Genesis, Exodus and so on. One of the guys took notice of what I was up to and approached my bunk where I lay on my back reading.

"Hey, Gilford, you actually reading the Bible from start to finish?" he asked.

"Yeah," I replied, "I never really read any of this, so I don't want to miss anything."

"You should really just skip right to the New Testament. The Old Testament might turn you off before you even get started. God did some pretty messed up stuff to those who misbehaved back before the New Covenant,"

"I appreciate the advice, but I gotta read it in order so I can make sense of it." "Okay", he snickered, "let me know how it goes when you get to Numbers and Kings." He chuckled as he walked off.

I understood his chuckling once I got to those and other chapters which seem to drone on and on about the lineage of King David. I stuck with it and was surprised to learn that so many phrases in our lexicon come from the Bible. "Rise and shine," and "by the skin of my teeth," to name a few.

Some of the fellas who saw what I was reading would occasionally ask if I'd like to join a group to read and discuss chapters, or to attend a service in the chapel, but I would always decline. I wanted to form my own opinions before I had other people's thoughts and biases influencing me. Also, I didn't want to have the views of one denomination or another doing the same. So, I stuck with my solitary journey of discovery. I was about halfway through the Old Testament when I received my sentence in a plea deal. Three years. I could have gotten as much as six had I taken it to trial, so I counted my blessings.

A short time later I was moved to the prison in Tracy, California where I waited for them to decide which prison I would end up in for the duration of my sentence. They actually had us fill out a questionnaire as to which prisons we would prefer in order to keep us close to family. The idea was that family ties help prevent convicts from re-offending and returning to prison. In actuality, prisoners are rarely sent to any of their three selections. As for me, I was to be sent to Norco, which is about as far from my home in Paradise, California as you could get.

While I awaited my transfer, I was placed in a cold, damp cell in the belly of a cell block on the ground floor. Sunlight barely hinted at penetrating the frosted glass on the other side of my barred window. The walls were painted tan and the lone fluorescent light bathed the cell in a sickly yellow light as it passed through the nicotine-stained plastic cover. It was depressing to say the least. When I got there, I found that I already had a cellmate who was reclining on his bottom bunk. As the heavy steel doors banged shut behind me, he sprang to his feet. What stood before me was a crazed looking old man of at least 60 years old. He had long scraggly gray hair, and liver spots that covered his hands and gaunt face. The really shocking feature on this guy was the fact that one of his nostrils had been torn off in some long-ago trauma! He had a bizarre look in his eyes. "Welcome, celly," he greeted me, "I'm Bigsby." He did a nervous little bounce and twitch as he spoke, which I'd soon become familiar with.

"Hi there, I'm Kevin," I said, eyeing him with suspicion as I dropped my meager belongings and began to put sheets on my bunk.

"You... You got any tobacco?" he twitched and bounced entirely too close to me as I tied the ends of my sheets together under the torn and stained mattress, an attempt to hold in the stuffing which was spilling out of all the tears the thing had.

"No, but I have some stamped envelopes. We could trade for some."

We were eventually able to procure some tobacco. An orderly who was let out of his cell to ostensibly sweep and mop the common area would spend most of his time brokering deals between the cells, no doubt making a tidy profit for himself along the way. The guards surely knew what was going on, but in their mind, they must have figured it kept the masses calm. Nobody wants a bunch of felons on edge. Bigsby turned to me as he retrieved our envelope of tobacco which had just been slid under our door by the orderly. "Got a light?" he asked, smiling with what I now saw was a single yellow tooth perched on the middle of his upper gums. *Ugh, this guy is gross!*

Our next conundrum was how to light our freshly rolled cigarettes. Bigsby had a solution to this. He dug a pencil out of a manila envelope and began gnawing on it with that lone tooth of his. It was disgusting to witness, but just fascinating enough that I couldn't turn away. Bits of wood and yellow paint began to litter his mouth and lips, some specks dropping to the floor of our cell. He eventually was able to extract a stick of graphite about three inches in length. He broke it into three pieces. Two of the pieces he stuck into each slot of the wall outlet. He then made a tiny rope out of tissue paper and tied it around the middle of the third piece, leaving graphite exposed at both ends. He held the rope with one hand, and a loose piece of tissue above the outlet with the other. He brought the ends of the graphite into contact with the pieces sticking out of the socket, and bang! With a flash of light, a loud spark, and a puff of smoke he had ignited the tissue, along with a bit of his hair. We quickly lit our smokes while the burning tissue scorched his blackened fingers. I laid on my top bunk to retreat into my reading, enjoying the carcinogens filling my lungs with comfort.

Once I was allowed to go to the commissary, I procured a big cylinder of Bugler tobacco, and we smoked to our hearts content.

I stuck with my game plan of reading the Bible cover to cover. It wasn't always easy trying to understand and retain what I was reading. Plus, I shared a cell with Bigsby, who cared not that I was immersed in reading and would just start bizarre conversations like we'd been talking to each other all along. Worse yet, I would sometimes be reading and feel his presence. I would drop my book to find his face inches from mine with that feral look on his face, "Can we have another smoke?" Of course, that was probably his normal face, but when it's suddenly right before you without hearing his approach, it's a frightening look!

I eventually made it past all the fire, judgment, and brimstone of the Old Testament, and began the journey into the New Testament. It immediately felt more real to me, like I was reading a history book. It felt like the truth. For the most part. There are some parts that continued to sound judgy to me, but I concentrated on the parts that felt right in my heart.

Often during the night, I would wake to find his silhouette framed by the night light that never went out, staring at me—a freaky sight! "Can we have a smoke?" he would always ask. "Dude, you can have a smoke whenever you want one. Don't fucking bother me when I'm sleeping! Or any other time, you dig?" I would snap. This scenario played out more than just a few times. I was beginning to think he was asking for a smoke to cover the fact that he was just staring at me while I slept! I only worried because I am such a heavy sleeper. I had no doubt I could take this old man in a fight, but it still gave me the willies!

One morning I awoke to the steel door to our cell slamming open the way it did each morning at six thirty, along with the announcement over the PA, "Chow Time."   I found that I wasn't feeling well. I couldn't put my finger on what it was at first, just that I felt like crap. So, I lay there a minute contemplating what was wrong. Bigsby was getting dressed. "You coming, bunky?" he asked as he twitched and bounced. I knew if I didn't go to breakfast I would have to wait until dinner for food, since they handed out lunch bags on our way out of the chow hall at breakfast. I dangled my legs over the edge of my bunk and slid on my belly until my feet touched the floor. Once I had all of my weight on my legs, I felt harsh pains shooting through my muscles and joints. I swooned as I tugged on my pants and slid my arms into my shirt. Bigsby led the way as we began our journey out of the cell and down the corridors to the chow hall. I felt lightheaded and strangely out of breath along the trek but kept up my pace with my fellow inmates. Along the way my plastic sandal slid off and scooted into the middle of the hallway, so I stepped out of line to retrieve it and caught a billy club in my left kidney from a screw for my trouble. "Stay in line, inmate!" he shouted at me. The blow dropped me to my knee, but I nevertheless collected my sandal and scurried back to the line like Quasimodo all hunched over. I was seeing stars but used the wall to steady myself as I walked.

I know I made it to the chow hall and back to my cell, but I have no memories of that space of time. I do remember being woken up for dinner, but I couldn't get up. My body felt as heavy as if it were made of lead and I couldn't take a deep breath. I rolled over away from the wall and let out a moan. Bigsby took one look at me and started bouncing and twitching like he was being electrocuted. "Oh man, you don't look good at all, man!" I could only moan in response. Bigsby darted to the open cell door, waved his arms, and shouted down to the CO's cage, "Help, this man needs help!" There was a steady stream of inmates walking past our cell on their way to dinner. They all gave a quick glance inside to see if there was any blood or carnage. Seeing none, they continued on their way. After getting no response from the guards, Bigsby left with the other inmates and alerted the guards to my condition.

Sometime later a hulking figure appeared in the doorway. "Inmate Gilford," he shouted, "have you taken any substances?" My thoughts were cloudy, and for a moment I wondered if Bigsby had slipped me something. "No," my voice came out weak and asthmatic. "On your feet, Gilford, I'll send you down to medical." I rolled onto my belly, swung my legs over the edge of my bunk and slid down slowly. When my feet hit the floor, electric shock waves shot through my legs and up into my chest. I saw stars again and was winded from the exertion. I stepped into my plastic sandals and shuffled out the door, hugging my arms against the chill that radiated across my skin.

Once we arrived at the gate to the cell block, the CO unlocked it, "Follow the blue stripe on the floor to medical, inmate," he instructed. I walked slowly down the corridors employing my earlier discovered method of leaning against the wall with my shoulder and sliding to help support my weight. When I came to an intersection or a doorway, I would have to fully support myself, which seemed impossibly hard. I arrived at another gated wall of bars, stopping my progress. I leaned my head against the cool bars which brought a modicum of relief to my feverish head. A CO eventually appeared on the other side of the gate. "Where you headed, inmate?" he barked at me. "Medical," I whispered, though I was trying to speak normally. After he radioed back to my cell block to confirm I was where I was supposed to be, he unlocked the gate so I could continue on my journey. "Inmate, push that book cart down to medical and leave it outside the door. I'll have someone come and get it from there," the guard ordered as I passed through to the other side. I saw before me a four-foot long, three-tiered behemoth of a cart loaded with heavy volumes. I leaned into it with all my weight and my foot immediately slipped out from my sandal as I tried to get traction. Once my sandal was back on, I again leaned into my cart. Slowly it began to move, but it took an extraordinary effort. Sweat began to pool under my arms, across my brow, and at the small of my back, but once I had got it up to speed, I was thankful I had it to lean on. The prison was massive, and I had to pass through several gates to reach my destination. Each time I had to stop, it got harder and harder to get the cart moving again. I kept seeing stars and felt as though I would faint throughout my journey, but I trudged on until I eventually arrived at medical. I parked the cart outside the door and collapsed in a chair just inside the waiting room.

Once the receptionist indicated it was my turn, I approached. Behind a plexiglass window with a circular pattern of holes drilled in the center, sat a middle-aged woman who wore a flower-patterned smock and a look on her face that let you know she'd seen some shit in her day, and she wasn't having any if it! "Name and complaint?" She snapped. "Gilford, I..,"

"Speak up, inmate!' she interrupted my raspy whisper. I inhaled as deep as I could to try and speak loud enough to be heard, but I saw stars and the room seemed to tilt. Everything went black.

When I came to, I was being put on a stretcher and wheeled into an examination room. A young doctor or medic came into the room just as the two orderlies who brought me in were leaving. She looked at my wrist band to get my name before addressing me. "Inmate Gilford, have you taken any substances in the past twenty-four hours?" I shook my head. "M-kay, you sure about that?" she asked the way your mom would when she knew you were lying. I shook my head again. She listened to my heart with her stethoscope and furrowed her brow. Then she listened to my lungs, again the furrowing of her brow. She spun around to grab that little finger device to measure oxygen levels and attached it to my index finger. Her eyes widened as she read the display. She snatched a radio from the desk and began giving orders. "Lori, call the hospital and tell them we need an ambulance, stat. We have an inmate with labored breathing, irregular heartbeat, and an oxygen saturation level of 62%. Also, call Lieutenant Iverson and tell him we have an inmate enroute to the hospital who needs an escort." She turned back to me, placed her hand on my arm and asked, "Gilford, you really need to tell me what you've taken so we can help you. Was it heroin, cocaine? Just tell me so we can help you"

"I...swear... I...haven't...taken...anything," I wheezed out, gasping for air between each word.

Soon I was being moved to a new stretcher brought in by two medics. Once I was on the thing, they cuffed my ankle to its frame and began to attach straps across my shins, thighs, and chest. They cinched them down so tight I couldn't move a muscle. I thought it was to prevent my escaping, but soon realized it was to keep me in the gurney as we left the exam room and headed down two flights of the steepest stairs I've ever seen.

Once we were in the ambulance and I was hooked up to an EKG, an IV, and had an oxygen mask secured over my mouth and nose, the questioning began. "Mr. Gilford, we gotta know what substances you've taken, otherwise we can't help you. I know you're worried about getting into more trouble than you already are, but you can't get in any more trouble than being dead." I tried to reply, but the mask and my labored breathing made it impossible, so I just shook my head no. He pulled a face that let me know he did not believe me, and that I had just made his job a lot harder.

Once we were in the emergency room, I found myself surrounded by a large crowd of doctors, nurses, and guards.

"Mr. Gilford, we're going to need to know what you've taken so we can help you out here buddy, capiche?" One of the doctors began as he checked my vitals. They must see a lot of this, I gathered.

"I...swear, I haven't...taken...anything."

"Okay then, were going to need a urine sample," the doctor informed me. As the doctor turned to grab a piss bottle, I suddenly realized I had to poop really bad. "I...gotta...poop"

"Ok, then. Nurse, grab a stool catcher."

I next found myself sitting on a toilet seat attached to a frame with a plastic bucket underneath it. I had a piss bottle poised over my dick, and there was an audience of about twelve encircling me waiting for me to shit and piss. So, there I sat with twenty-four eyes upon me. Now I have trouble doing my business when someone is in the stall next to me. With walls between us. The diarrhea was the easy part, no stopping that. The peeing took a bit of concentration. Funny, I had to pee very badly, but it just wouldn't happen in front of all these people. I closed my eyes and willed it to happen, imagining waterfalls and rushing streams. Eventually I felt a trickle seep into the container. I was able to squirt out enough for them to be satisfied. A nurse whisked away my offering, and back on the gurney I went.

The drug angle was put to rest once the results from my urine test came back negative for narcotics. The crowd mostly dispersed once the excitement was over, and I was taken to ICU. I was still struggling to breathe, though it was eased by the oxygen and some injection they'd given me.

My next trip took me to some room in the hospital that reminded me of Frankenstein's laboratory, with all kinds of machines and equipment filling the room. I was left there for some time, and I had drifted off to sleep. I was startled awake by a doctor who burst into the room, and with a booming voice announced, "Hi. I'm Ken with Nuclear Medicine." *What the what? Nuclear medicine? What the fuck is that?* I thought. "Mr. Gilford, I'm going to place this tube in your mouth. It's very important that you keep your lips sealed around the mouthpiece, breathe in through your mouth and only exhale through your nose. If this stuff goes directly from the tube, into the room before you breathe it in, it could damage my equipment," Ken explained it as if it shouldn't freak me out, but it did! "It's...safe...to...breathe, but...dangerous...for the...equipment?"

"Yep," was all I got in response as he placed the device in my mouth, made sure it had a good seal, and retreated to the safety of another room.

It took about thirty minutes of my sucking in God only knows what substance. Ken would come over the intercom periodically to remind me to keep my lips sealed over the mouthpiece and assure me it wouldn't be much longer. Once Ken got what he needed, he ran pure oxygen through the tube to flush out the lines before I could remove my lips from the mouthpiece. Once that was done, he dared to re-enter the room to unhook me from the contraption.

"Well, Mr. Gilford, it appears you have quite the double infection going on in your lungs. Your lower left lobe is the worst, it fills close to half the lung, but your right is only about a quarter affected," Ken explained as he wheeled my gurney over to a monitor where I was shown the images he captured.

I was taken to a special floor of the hospital for inmates and began taking a cocktail of antibiotics intravenously. There was a constant parade of phlebotomists, respiratory therapists, doctors, and nurses that came to poke, prod, and question me for the next two or three days.

My nurse was an angel. For the first time in a year, I had a person showing me compassion and tenderness, like I was a human being who needed and deserved care from another human being.

"How we doing today, hun?" she'd ask every time she began her shift. After she checked my vitals, wires and tubes coming and going from my body, she'd place her hand on my arm and look into my eyes and ask if there was anything I needed or wanted. Rarely did I have a request, so she'd find something to brighten my day a little bit. One time it was just getting the guard to loosen my ankle shackle. Another time she brought me a Coke. I wished I could've finished my sentence there!

It made me realize that I wouldn't always be judged by my faults or the transgressions of my past. Here was a person being kind to me while I was incarcerated. She had no idea what I had done to wind up in prison, and she didn't care! She was literally showing me how to put lessons from the Bible to use in real everyday life. "Judge not, lest ye be judged." "Do unto others as you would have others do unto you." and "love thy neighbor."

I don't recall how long I was in the hospital, but it was at least a week, maybe two, before I had to leave my sanctuary and go back to the prison.

When I got there, they allowed me to return to my old cell block to collect my belongings, even though I was to be moved to a new location. The turnkey allowed me to go to my old cell, which I found bolted shut. I found Bigsby alone in the cell. I tapped on the window and called his name. He sprung up from his slumber on the bottom bunk and immediately began twitching and bouncing about the cell. "Bigsby, where's my stuff, man?" I hollered through the door. He flailed his arms and paced back and forth while he gave his response. "They came... They took your stuff. I, I, I don't know what they did with it, brother." He twisted his fingers through his hair and pulled it back like he was facing impending doom, though for what reason I could not fathom. "Okay, later," I said, and left him gesticulating about the cell.

I made my way back to the guard cage and they soon realized that they had a bag of my stuff stashed in a nearby closet. I took a quick inventory of my life's possessions and found that my giant cylinder of Bugler tobacco was nearly depleted, which explained Bigsby's behavior. He'd smoked most of my tobacco, and knew he'd been caught. He probably figured I was dead anyways, so I silently forgave him.

I received orders from the guards to report to my new cell block and headed out across the compound, stopping every hundred yards or so at locked gates, where I had to give my name and destination. Each time took a good five to ten minutes for the gatekeeper to call in the information and confirm that it was correct. Along the way I was joined by two others heading to the same cell block. A six-foot Latino gentleman covered in gang tattoos on every inch of exposed skin. The number 13 was represented prominently on his face and on the backs of each hand. No doubt there were more hiding under his clothing. My other traveling companion was a punk. One who had been on hormones long enough to grow breasts. Quite a shock for this country boy, I can tell you that! She was about five foot even in height, had long curly blonde hair, and made a good case for the illusion of being a girl from birth.

When we got to the cell block and received our cell assignments, we entered the common area between the cells and the catcalls started immediately. Everyone else was locked in their cells, but she brought them all to their windows in their doors. "Okay, feather wood, I see you there."

"She can come be my bunky."

"Hey girl, I got what you need right here."

We split up at the stairs. I went up those on the right, she went to the left, and our Latino friend stayed on the ground floor. The catcalls continued, and I actually let out a chuckle when I heard someone yell, "Come on guys, that's another man's son you're hollering at! She's got a kickstand!"

The door to my new cell was cranked open, and before me stood my new celly. Just a normal looking middle-aged man who had two complete nostrils. *Thank God!* "Hi, my name is David." I shook his hand and introduced myself once I'd set down my bedding and other stuff.

David, it turns out, was a decent Christian man. He'd been out on parole for four years and had one glass of champagne at his daughter's wedding, which was against the rules of his parole. All would have been fine if he hadn't been pulled over for a broken taillight shortly after. The police officer smelled alcohol and gave him a breathalyzer, which he passed. However, there was a detectable amount of alcohol in his system, and when his PO caught wind of this, he was sent back to prison.

It was fortuitous for me, however, because having finally completed my reading of the Bible in its entirety, I was open to hearing other points of view on Christianity. I even went to some church services of differing denominations like Catholic, Evangelical and my favorite, Baptist. I say it was my favorite not because of the Baptist theology or doctrine, but because the minister was very animated.

"Gentlemen. Don't be discouraged because you are here in prison," he began as he circled to the front of his podium. "Be glad, for you're in good company. Jesus was a criminal too!" We all looked at each other nervously as he continued. "Yes, you should be remorseful for what you've done, and strive to better yourselves, and I'm sure that your crimes differ from that of Jesus, but the Lord loves those who repent and change their ways. When I say Jesus was a criminal, do you recall in Matthew 21:12, when he went into the temple and turned over the tables of the money lenders?" The preacher's voice rose to the point of yelling, and he grabbed a table, lifted the end, and let it drop with a bang. "Now that was criminal!"

That was one amazing sermon, I tell you! He really brought stories in the Bible to life for me, almost like watching a movie. It was through experiences like that, and my many conversations with David, that I began to believe in my heart that God has always been with me and wants me to be happy.

David helped me to see some of my less than Christian character flaws as well. One evening I had been telling him a story, and when I finished my rambling, he said to me, "Do you realize that you said the word 'fuck' five times in that last sentence alone?" Clearly, I had some work to do, but I was new to the faith and to trying to become a better person. So, I took the criticism in the spirit it was given.

I have to say that I don't just blindly believe every word in the Bible, and certainly not each sermon given by a pastor or priest. What I do believe is that I know in my heart when I read a passage that rings true. Things like believing and professing with your mouth that Jesus is Lord is the key to salvation. Loving one's neighbors. Doing unto others as you would have done unto you. These resonate with me, and I do my best to follow them.

I do not always hit the mark; I curse more than I should, and I don't always treat people as well as I could. However, I reflect on my actions daily and try to improve on my behavior.

My sudden illness that seemed to be a near tragedy, turned out to be a blessing. It got me away from Bigsby who may or may not have been plotting my demise each night while I slept. It brought me the tender caring I so desperately needed from my nurse, and it landed me with David who helped me to develop my faith. Non-believers will say these are all mere coincidences, but the feeling in my heart is that they are not. Realizing that, and believing God is with me, helped me immeasurably to endure hard times. Because I realize that you may never see the plan while you're going through something, but quite often once you've reached the other side and you look back, it becomes crystal clear, and you feel the hand of God!

Christianity helped me see my own self-worth, which had been missing since my spiritually void meth-man days. It was the nudge I needed to begin a more intentional life. A life in which I valued myself and others.

Chapter Eight

FACING YOUR FEARS

It was after a few months that my destination had been decided by the California penal system, and I was sent to a southern California joint in Norco. About as far away from home as you could get, and still be in the same state.

I was housed in a giant gymnasium converted into reception housing with hundreds of other poor souls like myself. We slept in triple decker bunk beds that stretched as far as the eye could see, barely enough room between them for one person to stand. I was unlucky enough to be assigned a middle bunk. It was wedged so close to the one above it that I could only lay on my back or on my stomach. If I wanted to turn over, I had to get out of bed and climb back in on my other side. There wasn't enough room to change my mind, let alone change positions.

I stayed in those accommodations for about a month before they moved me to my next place of residence, a 48-man dorm. Double bunks stretched along each wall of this long and narrow room, with a wide opening to a bathroom and shower area halfway down one wall, and a CO's office at the entrance to the dorm. That office had a big window so the goings on could be viewed with ease from a chair behind a desk.

For mealtimes we'd head down a series of corridors, down two flights of stairs, and down another long corridor to reach the chow hall. We did this twice a day—in the morning for breakfast when we'd pick up a box lunch to save for later, and once again for dinner. The cuisine was less than stellar as you can imagine. Breakfast alternated between oatmeal, which had the texture and taste of nearly hardened cement, and powdered eggs which were somehow both runny and powdery at the same time. The lunch box always had four slices of bread and an apple or orange, along with a pouch of fruit flavored drink mix. If you were lucky, you got tubes of peanut butter and jelly. Usually, you got mystery meat with packets of mustard and mayo. Dinners were mostly pasta with mystery meat, and to this day I can't even look at goulash or Hamburger Helper without feeling slightly ill. American chop suey? No thank you! Chicken was a big treat, but these poor leg quarters looked like they were harvested from anorexic and adolescent chickens. Every once in a great while we'd get a slice of cake, and if we were really lucky, there'd be frosting on top! Word had already reached our dorm that this was a frosted cake night when my next adventure began.

When we entered the chow hall the CO's would make us sit next to whomever we were next to in line. This was a problem because the unwritten prison rules dictated you weren't supposed to sit with other races at mealtimes. Not only that, but sitting next to punks, child molesters, or rats was a bigger no-no. Knowing who the punks were was easy, as they were very flamboyant. Other races were easy to spot as well, but being a newbie, I had no idea who may or may not be a rat or child molester.

During the trek to the chow hall everyone jockeyed for position next to who they wanted to sit with. It would always start before we left the dorm, like people of the same race bunching up together. Then once we were released for mealtime, final placement changes would be made. It wasn't a guarantee you'd wind up sitting next to the person you were next to in line, but it improved your chances to get in the middle of a good group of guys.

Now I have a wicked sweet tooth, and thoughts of this cake were at the forefront of my mind as I angled for a good position in line as we walked down the corridors. Just as we arrived at the entrance to the chow hall, I wound up in what seemed to be a good group. All White guys like me with plenty of prison tats. The guy right in front of me was perfect: plenty of tats and I'd seen him holding court in the dorm with a congregation of his sycophants during the few days I'd been at the dorm. The guy behind me in line was a burly looking dude with his own array of tats as well. Thick curly hair, no neck to speak of, and meat hooks for forearms and hands.

We moved slowly through the chow line, picking up our ready filled trays as we went. There was a little opening through a wall of stainless steel where the food service workers would slide out the trays at the end of a long line just before we entered the seating area. We never saw the workers loading the trays, that way, in theory, nobody could play favorites or sabotage a tray.

I watched as those slices of cake came out of the window for the guys in front of me, one after the other. Crusty corner piece, nice center cut, corner, corner, center. I calculated my chances of a nice middle piece as we went. Finally, my time came and bingo, a beautiful fat center cut piece with lots of frosting! My lucky day! We shuffled along as we entered the dining area, the CO's directing us to our tables all the while. I'd only just looked up from my delicious slice of heaven when I saw my prime dining partner be seated at the last place of a table. I was the first at an empty table, Meat Hooks sat at another place, and luckily two White guys filled out the last two seats. They looked sketchy, but Meat Hooks seemed unalarmed, so that was good enough for me. We all dug into our meals, knowing that we only had a few minutes before we'd be called to leave so the next group could be ushered in.

I was plowing through the "savory" portion of my meal, ready to abandon it in favor of that cake when a gravelly voice broke my concentration.

"Hey."

I looked up to see Meat Hooks looking at me. "You gonna eat that?" he asked. I wasn't sure what he meant, so I just looked at him dumbfounded for a moment. "I said, are you gonna eat that?" He asked as he extended his index finger and sunk it slowly, dirty nail and all, into my cake. I looked down at my defiled dessert while I considered my options. I'd already made one blunder with my *beat you off* fiasco, but I wouldn't have that kind of luck twice. If a physical altercation ensued, we wouldn't get far before the cops busted it up. If I backed down, my fate would be sealed, and I would be a bitch to anyone who wanted anything I had for the rest of my bid. I choked down my fear and took a leap of faith. I stuck out my own index finger, scrawny and pathetic compared to Meat Hook's kielbasa-sized digits, and I plunged it into his slice of cake, a crusty corner piece,

"Nah, I was going to eat this one," I said. My voice cracked when I said it, but I did get the words out. Meat Hooks held my gaze for what seemed like forever, then let out a roaring laugh. He continued to laugh as we kept our fingers inserted into each other's cake. After a moment or two he grinned at me while scooping up my cake. I did the same with his, and we kept our eyes locked as we crammed the sweetness into our mouths. "Pick it up," came the announcement from the CO's, and we, in unison, picked up our trays and began the file past the trash cans, to the tray depository, and back to our dorms.

I was a bit of a celebrity back at the dorm for a few days after that little escapade. It was one of the scariest things I'd ever had to do, but it paid dividends. Meat Hooks was amused and impressed with my bravery and treated me well from that point on.

Facing my fears has always been difficult, if not impossible, throughout my life. As I wrote in my journal that night, I reflected on how this was one of the scariest things I'd ever had to face, and how exhilarating and rewarding it was to have come out the other side alive and better for it. Usually, my fears are not so defined with black and white consequences staring me in the face.

One such time was when I had to have a difficult conversation later in life with my grandmother, who'd been psychologically tormenting my mother, her primary caregiver. My mother did everything for her. She took her grocery shopping every day, because that's what Grandma was used to doing since the days before refrigerators. She took her to lunch every day, though my mom could scarcely afford it, because that's what Grandma wanted. Mom even had to clean up after her whenever she'd had an accident.

Yet Grandma was constantly tormenting my mother with her passive aggressive nature, accusing her of not caring whether she lived or died, and suggesting she was out having all sorts of fun without her.

It all came to a head shortly after Mom had an accident and totaled her car. Mom decided right then and there that she was done driving, telling me that "old people shouldn't be allowed to drive." Though mom was only in her sixties at the time, she was adamant, and I picked up the shopping duties from then on.

One time when I took the two ladies to the grocery store, which I had insisted be only once a week, Grandma had a tantrum over whether or not she should ride in the electric buggy or just hold onto the handle of the shopping cart for support. Grandma had been very unsteady on her feet that day, and we were able to convince her to use the buggy, but she gave Mom the silent treatment for making her feel old. She wouldn't answer Mom as to what groceries she wanted or needed and would scoff at any selections that we made for her.

When we had got back to her apartment and Mom was putting Grandma's groceries away, I sat Grandma down in a chair and kneeled beside the chair so that I could be at eye level with her.

"Grandma, you know I love you, but you cannot treat my mom the way you did today. We are both trying extremely hard to take care of you and give you everything you need. If you treat my mom like you did today, you'll never go shopping again, do you understand me? I will simply drop off whatever I think you might need and there will be no more shopping, going to lunches, or anything."

She apologized immediately and we both cried a little bit. I looked into the kitchen where my mom had been listening to the conversation and I saw her mouth the words, "thank you" with tears streaming down her face. Grandma didn't make a complete transformation after that, but she surely was a better version of herself.

None of these were as scary as the consequences I had faced with Meat Hooks, but scary just the same, and I attribute my ability to face them back to moments like that. My fears in prison were of physical brutality at the hands of inmates and screws alike. I was in survival mode.

Out of prison, the risks were not so physical or immediate, nut I've channeled my experiences to address my fears or discomfort. I've become more confident in my ability to rise to challenges.

Chapter Nine
MS. CHERRY

My time was getting relatively short at the CRC-Norco, California joint that had been my home for the last two years. I had been working on a crew that fought forest fires in the areas surrounding the prison, a great privilege with lots of perks, but had been taken off that job after it was discovered that I still had an outstanding warrant for my arrest. They had this funny rule about not letting anyone outside of the prison gates with charges hanging over their heads. So, I had been reassigned as a cook in the mess hall, and Ms. Cherry was the screw in charge.

Ms. Cherry hated Mexicans. Probably still does if she's alive after all these years. And it didn't matter if they were Guatemalan, Dominican, or Columbian. To her they were all Mexicans.

Ms. Cherry was a Black woman in her mid-fifties, and she always referred to herself in third person. "Ms. Cherry wants this food cooked her way. Ms. Cherry don't take no bow-shit!" Her all-time favorite phrase was, "You treat Ms. Cherry right, Ms. Cherry treat you right." It was true, Ms. Cherry did treat you right. As long as you treated her right, and as long as you weren't Mexican!

Now Ms. Cherry's way of talking wasn't her only noteworthy aspect; her appearance was something straight out of a Carol Burnett sketch. She was tall, maybe six feet, mostly legs with a short torso. She had a way of walking hunched over that made her big butt stick up higher than her belly button. Her belt seemed to be secured directly under her enormous cone shaped breasts, as if to keep them from sliding down her front. Upon that belt swung a walkie talkie, keys, and the ever-present panic button. This button looked like a garage door opener, and once pressed, it would summon the "Goon Squad." The Goon Squad was a group of hulking CO's that would come running with astonishing speed whenever the alarm was sounded. Their first order of business when they'd arrive would be to beat any and all prisoners to the ground and pummel them into submission until it was determined that they no longer posed a threat. Questions could wait until later. Ms. Cherry loved to threaten to push the button at any real or perceived defiance from an inmate. She'd tap the button lightly with her index finger like Doc Holiday ready to draw and ask, "We got a problem with Ms. Cherry? Cause Ms. Cherry can settle it!" Upon her head sat both a wig and a correctional officer's ball cap. Both worn askew, and in opposite directions. Every day was a different wig, and each day it was worn off center. Like didn't this woman even own a mirror? Beneath that wig dangled giant gold hoop earrings, and her lips were painted in what I'd call hooker red. The red of those lips seemed all the more absurd in contrast to her incredibly dark skin. Skin which was beautifully smooth and without wrinkle or blemish. If it weren't for the jaundice in the whites of her eyes, the crackly voice, and the slouched gait, one would be hard pressed to guess her age.

All jobs in the prison had to be racially diverse between Blacks, Whites, and Hispanics. "Other" was a term given to any who fell outside the big three races and were an afterthought. They took whatever jobs were given to them. Here in the kitchen, we had two Whites: a fella called Tommy Gun and me. Tommy was a skinny biker type with long dirty-blonde hair, lots of tattoos, and very few teeth. Clearly a tweaker. Two Blacks: Chris, an enormous kid who'd most likely worked his way into the kitchen job for ulterior motives. Then we had a "Jafaken" who called himself Bumbadee. A lean dark-skinned brother from San Bernardino who affected a Jamaican accent for reasons only he understood. Our two Mexicans were Spider and LRG. Spider was a veteran of many prison bids as evidenced by the tattoos that covered his body from face to fingertips. Teardrops under his eyes, spider webs on his elbows and bones on the back of his digits—classic prison tats. Somehow, he had risen to the position of head cook in Ms. Cherry's fiefdom. LRG stood for "Little Round Guy," a name given him by Spider on his first day, which happened to be my first day as well. LRG was as sweet a guy as you would hope to meet on the inside. He was soft-spoken, funny, and considerate. He stood maybe five feet tall and seemed just as wide. From his pillowy jowls to his Jell-O like mid-section, he was a living teddy bear, and Ms. Cherry hated him from the moment he walked through her door. She was relentless in her criticism of him and rode him like a rented mule. She followed him around that kitchen inches from his backside, yapping in his ear, "Ms. Cherry told you not to pour that so fast. Stir that slowly. Don't open that. Close that!" And she always ended each sentence with, "You treat Ms. Cherry right, Ms. Cherry treat you right!" The guys in the kitchen would exchange awkward glances as she matched him step for step around the kitchen each day, berating his every move. We knew nothing or no one could rescue him or divert her attention for more than a moment.

One day Ms. Cherry called me into her office and told me she liked the way I worked and knew from my file that I had cooked in restaurants on the streets. "Ms. Cherry wants to know if you think you can handle the lead cook position?"

I wanted to ask, "What about Spider?" but knew better so I replied, "Of course." "Ms. Cherry thinks there might be an opening soon. You treat Ms. Cherry right, Ms. Cherry treat you right. Now keep this under your hat for now." I recall thinking as I left her office that Spider had always seemed exempt from her hatred, never receiving the same treatment as LRG, but I wasn't considering the most important fact: he was a Mexican!

Over the course of the next few days Ms. Cherry's treatment of LRG was as relentless as always, but still she showed no signs of hostility towards Spider. LRG's demeanor was that of a beaten man as she continued to harass him. His eyes were downcast, shoulders slumped, and voice timid in any and all communication he had with any who spoke to him. He was steadfast in his humility and politeness no matter how abusive Ms. Cherry was to him. "Yes, Ms. Cherry. No, Ms. Cherry. Whatever you say, Ms. Cherry," was the way he addressed her, and all this seemed to do was to fuel her anger.

One day Ms. Cherry, in a surprising show of charity and kindness, baked a sheet of chocolate chip cookies and placed them on a table in the kitchen for us. "Come get yourselves a cookie. Like I always say, you treat Ms. Cherry right, Ms. Cherry treats you right." As she peeled a cookie off the sheet and took a bite, she looked at me and gave me a wink so slight I couldn't be sure I saw it. I took the gesture to be nothing more than Ms. Cherry being in a kind and friendly mood, a side of Ms. Cherry I'd never seen during the few months I'd been in her kitchen. As she walked back to her office, cookie in hand, we hesitated, giving each other uncertain glances before Chris broke the spell and grabbed the first cookie. The rest of us followed suit and gathered around the cookie sheet and took our treats. As we each savored our first bites of warm and gooey heaven, our faces lightened with the joy we were experiencing. I had been locked up for over a year and a half by now. The other guys, just as long, if not longer. This was like a taste of home, of freedom. Chris reached for another cookie before Spider stopped him. "Wait. Did she say we could have two?" Chris's voice rose a few octaves as he reasoned, "Yo, she said come get some cookies." "Nah mon, she say have 'a' cookie," Bumbadee retorted. We all struggled to recall her exact verbiage, but none of us had the wits to just go and ask Ms. Cherry to clarify if we were allowed a second cookie. Chris counted the cookies. "Look, guys. There's six left. We ate six and Ms. Cherry ate one. That's a total of thirteen, a baker's dozen. Everyone knows there's thirteen in a baker's dozen so the baker can taste one to be sure it's good. That means she left the rest for us. What else could it be?" He raised his arms from his side and shrugged his shoulders. There were no other workers in the kitchen. In the dining and scullery areas there were fifteen or so inmates working—too many for the few cookies left. There was no poking any holes in Chris's theory, so we eagerly scooped up our second cookie and chomped away with glee.

We'd all gone back to our respective tasks: Spider was stirring a giant steam pot with a stainless steel paddle shaped like an oar, LRG was laying biscuits out on a massive cookie sheet, Chris and Bumbadee were chopping vegetables, while I began setting up the serving line. The flavor of those cookies was still lingering in my mouth as I went about my job. Tommy Gun must have been in the freezer getting boxes when Ms. Cherry strolled into the kitchen and stopped at the table with the empty cookie sheet laying on it. I was watching from the corner of my eye as she bowed her head and stared at the few remaining crumbs scattered on the pan. She let out a strong and steady breath, then snapped her head towards LRG who had his back to her. "How many cookies did you have?" She asked accusingly. We all spun around to face her, including LRG. She was slightly nodding her head as she repeated, "I said, how many cookies did you eat?" LRG gave us each a quick pleading glance. I could tell what he was thinking, that we'd all had two cookies, but he couldn't dry snitch by saying that. He knew it would not save him even if he did. "What you looking at them for, you need them to remind you of how many you had?" She shouted. "N-n-no Ms. Cherry, I had two," he replied sheepishly, lowering his head in defeat. Spider tried to intercede but was cut off before the first syllable escaped his mouth. Ms. Cherry held her hand up to Spider as she began yelling at LRG. "Who told you could have two cookies? You people are all alike: greedy! Can't be grateful for what you got; you always have to have more!" She circled around the table as she moved in on her prey "Ms. Cherry treat you right, but you don't treat Ms. Cherry right!"

It was like watching Thelma and Louise speeding towards the cliff and you knew nothing could stop the calamity. She came to a stop directly in front of LRG as she berated him with her nonstop diatribe, her massive cans nearly in contact with his lowered head.

His head stayed down only shaking slightly back and forth as she continued her verbal assault. He looked all the more pathetic with his arms hanging slack by his sides, giant oven mitts covering his hands and forearms. The rest of us remained frozen. Tommy Gun appeared in the doorway carrying a large box, stopped when he saw what was unfolding, then slowly backed away, disappearing from view. *Lucky bastard*!

When LRG finally broke, it sent a mixture of both fear and relief through me. She was repeating her famous line for the umpteenth time, "You treat Ms. Cherry right, Ms. Cherry treat you right!" That was the last straw. LRG flung his oven mitts to the ground, balled up his fists, looked Ms. Cherry in the eyes and said, "Lady, if you don't shut the fuck up, I'm gonna treat you to a right, and a left!" Spider took a half step toward them, to restrain LRG no doubt, but checked himself mid-stride. Ms. Cherry's face broke into a Cheshire grin. "Gotcha" was her victory cry as she pointed her index finger at him, then slowly brought it down to hit the panic button.

Someone uttered, "Shit!" just before the alarm sounded, and almost immediately after came the thundering of approaching boots. We all knew the drill, so we dropped flat on our stomachs, clasped our fingers behind our heads and prepared for the beatings. We didn't have to wait long; the Goon Squad flooded the room as pandemonium ensued. I felt the wind rush from my lungs as a heavy body landed upon my back, knee first! My face bounced off the concrete floor. Stars flooded my vision as the metallic taste of blood flooded my mouth. My limbs were contorted to receive the shackles around my wrists and ankles.

My comrades were faring no better and we were eventually dragged to a seated position, lined up against a wall in the dining area. I looked to my right and left to see the battered faces of not only the kitchen crew, but the servers and dishwasher guys as well. They were oblivious to the reasons for their predicament, as they were in other parts of the mess hall tending to their duties when it all went down. I saw split lips, bloody noses, scuffed foreheads and one poor dude with a trickle of blood coming out of his ear. We were a motley looking crew for sure.

Ms. Cherry walked up with two goons flanking her. She continued down the line of human misery until she came to LRG. "This one here threatened me with physical violence, and this one," she pointed to Spider, "was coming to back up his homie when I hit the button!"

With that, it was all over for our Mexican friends Spider and LRG. Two birds with one stone. It was clear that Ms. Cherry had been at this game a long time, and she knew all the tricks of the trade.

The next day the replacements walked through the door. Two Mexicans of course (have to keep the racial diversity equal), but at least in Ms. Cherry's eyes they'd be at the bottom of the food chain now that I'd been made head cook and my coworkers had all moved up in rank. The new guys had the look of lambs being led to the slaughter; word of yesterday's events had clearly spread. Ms. Cherry's reputation was becoming legendary.

Ms. Cherry began her orientation, "All you fellas need to know about this job is if you treat Ms. Cherry right........."

My entries into my journal that night centered on prejudice. Hate in all its forms, be it racism, bigotry, or what have you, doesn't need to be based in any reason. Sometimes people just hate, and there's no logic that can sway its course. Now I'm not a big conspiracy theory guy, even after this, but people will conspire to achieve their goals.

Had I not had that meeting with Ms. Cherry a few days before the incident, I would have thought Spider was just collateral damage. Spider had told me when I first started in the kitchen that Ms. Cherry hated Mexicans, but I thought it was just his overactive imagination. After all, Spider was head cook, and was treated very well by Ms. Cherry, but her true colors revealed themselves over the course of these events.

Another nugget I walked away with is that opportunity sometimes comes when it is somewhat undeserved. In this case I was certainly qualified, but did I deserve it? It's certain that Spider didn't deserve to lose it. Not to mention going to the SHU and probably losing some good time. Maybe worse. I never found out.

I've benefited many times in my life from being in the right place at the right time, or just being liked more than a person more deserving. Usually in the workplace. I repeatedly made the cut during layoffs at a job I had when the company rules specifically stated that seniority was to be the determining factor. While at that same job, I got a promotion to a leadership position role over a much more qualified person who'd been at the company for much longer than I had. I felt bad for the guy. He'd been preparing his whole life for this job, had gone back to school to get his degree and was much more knowledgeable than me. However, I was well liked by management, mostly because of my positive attitude and general work ethic.

The fella I beat for the job came to my office one day in tears, "I just don't understand how you got this job, Kevin. I've been here for over twenty years, I got my degree, and here you are, an ex-felon with a GED! Don't get me wrong, you're a great guy and I think you'll do a good job, but I deserve it!"

I couldn't bring myself to tell him that he just wasn't well liked, so I just told him people loved being part of a redemption story: ex-con makes good and all that. I honestly believed that was true, though not the whole truth. The universe has a way of balancing the scales though, and I've missed out on opportunities that could have gone my way. Thankfully, I'm at a place in my life now where I can recognize and accept that this is how life goes and be at peace with it. Thankful for the blessings I do and have had.

Chapter Ten

WORDS MEAN DIFFERENT THINGS TO DIFFERENT PEOPLE

I WOULD LIKE TO be able to tell you that I left prison with my newfound spirituality and knowledge from the lessons I'd learned on the inside, righted all my wrongs, and went on to lead an exemplary life from that point on. However, as you know by now, I have to learn things the hard way.

I had been out for several years and had been able to earn my GED, hold down a steady well-paying job, and basically become a reasonably responsible guy. I had moved to New Hampshire to be closer to my mother who had moved there several years prior. I had found work and an apartment, and all seemed to be going well. However, the drug that had held me captive for so long had not let go of me yet; it had merely loosened its grip.

I had found myself in some dire financial straits and decided the best way out was to fire up the meth lab again to bail myself out. It went about as well as you'd expect. After all, I always got caught!

While responding to an alarm I'd set off while cooking dinner one night, the fire department found my meth lab in a closet, and quick as you please, I was back on the inside.

My final tour began in the local county jail. I had been sampling the product, of course, to be sure of its quality, so when I arrived in county, I slept for a few days solid. The other inmates would call to me in my cell to see if I wanted dinner, but I just needed sleep. One night I heard someone calling me by name from the door to my cell and when I answered, the gentleman exclaimed, "It *is* you! You all over the news, bro!" I silently cursed my stupidity, felt an excruciating shame for my mother's sake, and rolled over to escape back into the void of sleep.

I eventually could sleep no longer and emerged from my cave, made the most painful of all phone calls ever to Mom, and began assimilating myself back into incarcerated life.

It was at about four months in that I began to learn that not all prisons across this great land of ours had the same set of unspoken rules about doing time.

My bunky and I were playing cards against a pair of other fellas. One of our opponents, Jake, had been there since I'd arrived. He was a young guy, probably in his early twenties. Nice enough guy, just a bit rambunctious and green around the edges. His partner Mike was a new arrival to our pod, but evidently familiar to the regulars in the county system. Mike was a bragger, the type that portrayed himself as a hardened criminal, savvy in all the ways of doing time. I hated him immediately.

Before we all sat down to the game, I asked Mike about his scar which traversed from one ear, across the crown of his skull, and down past his other ear. It was plain to see since he was only about five-feet-five inches tall. I stand five-feet-ten, so I had a clear line of sight to this distinguishing remnant of a past trauma. "Bone cancer. I had to have surgery when I was just a kid. My hair never grew back to cover it," he told me. Later, another guy pulled me aside and whispered in my ear. "He's full of shit. He got his head split open by a baseball bat when he tried screwing someone in a drug deal."

So, we began playing cards. Spades was the game since none of these county boys had the intellect to manage pinochle. The trash talking started early in the game as it tends to do. Nothing too heavy, just a "whooped you on that round," and "don't put your kids in the street, they'll get run over," type of friendly banter.

Then Mike beat me on a round and bragged, "Took you to task on that one, punk!" I sprang to my feet, knocking my chair over behind me in the process. "What'd you call me, motherfucker? I'll make you eat those words!"

"Whoa, take it easy, killer. We're just having a friendly game here." Mike said, appearing to regret his words, but then probably fearing he would look weak, he followed up with, "So sit down *punk!*" I circled the table and punched him in the square in the nose! I felt a satisfying crunch of cartilage as he fell back onto the floor. I chased him down as he fell and rolled away from me. As he went to rise, I moved in for another shot, but my plastic jailhouse sandal blew out and I fell to the floor. He jumped on top of me and began swinging, the blood from his nose streaming down onto my face. I was able to grasp him by the shoulders, and since his arms were so short, he couldn't land any punches. Our fellow inmates had the whole thing broken up before the deputies could get there, but soon enough we were both sitting in separate holding cells.

"Okay, Mr. Gilford, care to explain what happened in there?" Deputy Larson asked after I had a chance to settle down.

"He called me a punk. I gave him a chance to apologize and take it back, but he doubled down and called me a punk again."

"Am I missing something here? What's wrong with being called a punk?"

"Are you serious? How long have you been working here? A punk is someone who blows guys and takes it in the shitter! You can't let an accusation like that slide on the inside. Your life will be a living hell if you do!"

"Well, that *is* a serious accusation, I've never heard the term used that way before," was all I got in response.

The deputy left the cell and I laid back on the concrete bench to contemplate what repercussions I could expect from this and replayed the events in my head. I relished the fact that I had gotten in one good blow and hadn't received any in the fight, something I rarely accomplished; I usually blocked punches with my face.

Larson later returned with a bemused look on his face. "Well Mr. Gilford, funny story, it turns out the term 'punk' doesn't mean what you think it means. At least not here."

"Mike's just trying to fool you into thinking he didn't provoke me. It's cool, I take all the blame," I told him.

"Well, I thought of that. So, I went to your pod and asked all the guys there what they thought 'punk' meant, and each of them thought it was nothing more than being called a jerk, basically. All the deputies say they never heard the term used that way either. Your fellow inmates were all surprised you reacted that way, until I told them what your definition was." I was stunned. It was common knowledge back in California!

It was then that I decided to get back into journaling, taking daily stock of my actions and words, and try and find my way back to the person I had so briefly become.

I had the realization that different regions and different people have varying meanings for words. Especially when those words are used in slang. I was going to have to be more observant and take the temperature of the room before reacting in the future.

Chapter Eleven

FRIENDLY PEOPLE AREN'T ALWAYS YOUR FRIENDS

I WAS MOVED FROM county jail to a Concord, New Hampshire prison once it was determined that my case was to be taken over by the Feds. There I would await a trial for my most recent crimes. I was being housed along with eleven other guys in a reception area of the joint. These were two-man cells with cinder block walls on three sides and a barred wall and door at the front of the cell. The cells were about three feet wide and eight feet in length. All the cell doors faced in the same direction, out onto the walkway, so none of us could see one another.

We were locked down all day except for one hour of yard time, and for mealtimes. The only thing we had to occupy our days were writing and reading letters, and a book cart that was full of crappy novels that usually had more than just a few pages missing.

I had a fat celly named Gonzo who was quite possibly the most disgusting individual I had ever met. He had an ungodly body odor that never seemed to go away, even right after showering. I wondered if he used soap. He clearly suffered from some sort of digestive issues, and since our toilet/sink combo was in our tiny cell, I bore the full brunt of its effects while I lay upon my bunk. I would pull my blanket over my head and hold my deodorant up to my nose while he did his business.

Aside from his smell, the snoring and farting, and of course the bowel movements, at least he was a nice guy. He was in prison for habitually driving on a suspended license. I thought it a bit much to be sent to prison for such an offense, but hey, that's our justice system.

I had gotten to know a little about the other residents on our block during yard and mealtimes. A regular bunch of convicts: most were there on drug charges, one guy for bank robbery, and another for some check cashing scheme.

The most memorable one out of the group was Marcus. He was a Black guy, in his mid-thirties. He was only about five-foot-five, but he was lean and muscular, and I had no doubt he could handle himself in a fight.

Marcus had the gift of gab, and he made it his pastime to get to know everyone's story of how we'd gotten there. Now most people tend to fib a little to add some color and intrigue to their stories, and Marcus had a clever way of poking holes in their stories and bringing the truth to light. Usually it was nothing earth shattering, just inflating the amount of drugs or money involved to make themselves seem a little bit cooler than they really were.

"What about you, country, how'd you get here?" he asked me at yard time one day.

"Country, why do you call me that?" I asked. I wasn't offended, I just didn't get the reference.

"Your accent. Where you from, Texas?"

"Funny, everyone since I got to New Hampshire seems to think I came from Texas. No, I'm from Northern California."

"No shit? What charge did you catch?"

I'd seen him go down this road enough times to know exactly where it was headed, but I was wary of talking about my case since I was still awaiting trial. "Manufacturing methamphetamines. My name is Kevin Gilford. I got busted back in February of this year. I'm still awaiting trial so I'm afraid I can't discuss my case, but it was in all the papers, so if you want to know more about it, you'll have to find out that way."

That satisfied Marcus, and he was off to chat up some other guy. I saw what he was doing, and frankly appreciated it very much. He was making sure that we didn't have any rats or pedophiles in our midst. The last thing you wanted was to become friendly with someone, only to find out later you'd been seen chumming it up with one of these types.

One day while we were all locked in our cells, a newbie arrived. The guards marched him past Marcus's cell and put him in a cell between his and mine. Since mine was the last one in the row, I didn't get a look at him. I heard Marcus ask the guard, "Who's this? What's he in for?"

"You'll find out," was the whispered response from the guard. Now Marcus asked this question every time they brought someone new in, and this was the first time there had been any response at all. Marcus moved in for the kill.

"Hey, new guy. What's your name, man?" No reply came. "Carl, tell your bunky I'm talking to him," Marcus called over.

"Dude, he's talking to you" I heard from next door.

"Jack. I don't really feel like talking right now," came the hesitant response.

"Jack. You the one I read about in the paper. You the one that was messing with those kids, right?" Marcus persisted. A heavy silence hung in the air. Jack may as well have confessed on the spot; silence speaks louder than words.

I had no idea how this was going to play out, but I perked up on the edge of my bunk. Even Gonzo arose from his perpetual slumber.

Marcus took a tack I did not see coming. "It's cool man. You're among friends. We all in here for the same shit. You don't think they would've put you in with the regular convicts; that'd be a death sentence!" I could tell Jack was dubious in his reply.

"I—No, you got me mixed up with someone else."

"Nah, it's you man. Listen, we ain't none of us going nowhere for a long time. All we got is our stories, man, the memories. Look, I'll tell you what I used to do. I had a camera and a pocket full of candies. I would go to the playground and wait for the moms to get distracted. That's when I'd move in and try and disarm them, tell them I wanted to take their picture. Sometimes I would tell them I was an agent for TV. Then I'd get them in the bushes where no one could see us." My jaw was on the floor. I thought Marcus was spinning tales, but it sounded too legit!

Marcus's story must have gotten the pervert's juices flowing, and he couldn't help himself. "I was too afraid to do what you did. It was my neighbor's kid. She'd asked me to babysit her eight-year-old once in a while. At first I..."

I'm not going into details on how Jack's story continued, but suffice it to say it was disgusting! He deserved what happened when they opened our cell doors the next time.

I would have had no qualms about assisting in the beating that Jack took that day, but by the time I slid off my bunk and made it out onto the walkway, the melee was in full force. The guards took their time breaking it up, I have to say. I've seen many prison fights over the years and had never seen one last as long as this one did.

Friendly people aren't always your friends. Marcus skillfully disarmed ol' Jack in this instance, cozying up to him and making him feel safe in letting his guard down. It worked in favor of what I would call "prison justice" that time.

Sometimes the friendly ones are really the ones trying to hide something. When I got to the Fort Dix, New Jersey prison later that year I was immediately approached by a guy in the first dorm they'd put me in. He was way too friendly, and he made my Spidey senses tingle. He was either trying to seduce me or make friends to help him blend in and add credibility to himself. The jig was up when I asked him what he was in for. "Uh, computers," was the reply.

"Last time I checked, computers weren't illegal. You tried hooking up with a minor over the internet, didn't you?" His face flushed and he immediately went to turn himself into the SHU.

You run into these people in your daily life too, like when that coworker who normally doesn't give you the time of day is suddenly so interested in everything that's happening in your life. Next thing you know, anything you told them is all anyone can talk about at work.

Another simple edict that was reinforced by Bed Head is simply don't lie. The truth will always come out eventually. Besides, when you tell the truth, you never have to remember which lie you told to whom.

In the joint I would never be evasive about my charges, but I would try and never get too chummy with anyone until I was sure of their bone-fides first. So like Jow Friday would say, "Just the facts."

Chapter Twelve

IF YOU CAN'T BE HAPPY WITH NOTHING, THEN NOTHING CAN MAKE YOU HAPPY

Being incarcerated doesn't just mean losing your freedom, your possessions and contact with your loved ones. You lose your dignity, your basic rights, your privacy, and so much more. It can be soul crushing if you let it, and some people never learn to deal with it.

Before this, I could never get enough to feel complete or satisfied. There was never enough money, drugs, sex, or any number of possessions that could bring me comfort. It wasn't until I stopped trying to fill the void with stuff and started filling my soul with love that I found happiness. Real hippie sounding shit, I know, but it's true.

Spending time with my loved ones and sharing in their lives are my most cherished things. It's been over nineteen years since my final prison bid began, and today I have lots of nice possessions: beautiful home, a new car, and many truckloads of things that any person could want in life. My wife and I just bought a new home and the many truck loads being moved helped to fuel this chapter. It made me appreciate all these possessions of course, but also reminded me that if it were all gone tomorrow, I would still be happy.

It was early in the 2000's and I had only been at Fort Dix for a day or two. I hadn't been issued my allotment of clothing yet, so I was running around in a thin jumpsuit, a windbreaker and boat shoes in the middle of a frozen New Jersey winter the likes of which they rarely see in that region. I only had to cross an access road to get to the chow hall three times a day, so I didn't mind all that much. Mostly I just stayed in my dorm in the reception building and read my books and my Bible. The buildings were brick walls with concrete floors and were so drafty I could watch the blanket I would curl up with rustling in the breeze. Still, I was happy to be here after a month in Brooklyn, where simple comforts like salt or access to books were nonexistent. I knew it wouldn't be long before I had a nice jacket and knit hat like the rest of the population, so I suffered with confidence that this was as bad as it was going to get.

It was the middle of the night when the alarm sounded. I could hear CO's marching down the hall shouting for everyone to exit the building. I was still rubbing the sleep from my eyes when the door to our dorm burst open, the light was switched on and a screw began barking orders at us. I got dressed and wrapped my blanket around my shoulders so I wouldn't freeze outside, but the CO stopped me before I reached the door and said, "Lose the blanket inmate!"

"I don't have a coat," I explained. "Should have thought of that before you got caught committing a crime!" he retorted. Defeated, I shrugged off the blanket and fell in line with my cellmates on our trek to the frozen tundra.

I was prepared for the cold, the wind, and even the snow on the ground which promised to saturate my thin canvas shoes and soak my socks. Yet I was utterly stricken with horror when we reached the outside to find that we were in the middle of a freezing rain stormageddon! The wind was so strong that the freezing rain felt like ice needles flying horizontally into my face, legs, and torso! To further our torment, we were lined up in rows for head count, not on the plowed pavement of the road that ran along the front of our building, but along the side of the structure where a lawn presumably lay dormant under a half a foot of snow and ice.

I tried to huddle up closer to the guy in front of me in line to block the wind and rain, but the gusts switched direction and left me unprotected. I tried jogging in place to increase blood flow, but my overweight body and smokers' lungs could only manage a few moments before I became winded and dizzy. My next attempt at relief was to stand on one foot for a count of thirty before switching feet, but I wasn't sure if it was colder for my foot to be in contact with the frozen ground, or exposed to the arctic wind, so I just a performed a combination of all the above in rapid succession in what must have looked like a man being shocked by the earth while simultaneously being attacked by bees! Even my compadres who were lucky enough to have jackets and hats appeared as miserable as me. And here I thought all my problems could be solved by a few more layers!

The alarm continued to sound while the screws came by in pairs to count and double count our huddled masses. They wore thick jackets and scarves, heavy boots, and Russian style fur hats. I've never been so envious in all my life!

I'm not sure if being able to count is a requirement for the job of CO, because they never seemed to get it right. Every two or three minutes a pair would make a circuit around our ranks, gloved fingers pointing at our heads while their lips silently mouthed the numbers they were adding. Each time they came out of the warm building to count, and then returned to tally the numbers. It must have been five attempts at simple math before they sent out the replacements to try and bring in a correct count, and still that fucking alarm wailed! These buffoons were no better than their predecessors, and I could tell from their lips that they were mouthing completely different numbers as they strode by, poking their gloved fingers in our direction.

I felt like I was going to lose my mind! My extremities had gone from cold, to numb, to painful pins and aches while I shivered uncontrollably! I mean, come on, how hard is it to count a few hundred guys already? We were all lined up in neat rows of quivering ranks! There was no way that somebody had escaped from this prison of brick walls, steel doors, and rows of chain link fences topped with absurd amounts of coiled razor wire. There was a pathway about six feet wide between two fences and even that was filled with razor wire from the ground to the tops of those twelve-foot-high barriers! Tax dollars at work.

Eventually the alarm fell silent, and the inmates let out a collective sigh of relief. Much to our chagrin, however, when the CO's came back out from the building, they did not instruct us to return to our dorms. Those fiends began the count ritual all over again! And again! And again!

I can't say with any certainty how long we actually had to endure our torture before they allowed us to return to our dorms, but I'm sure you can imagine it felt like an eternity. When we made it back to our dorm, we found a mountain of what had been our individual possessions, now piled in the center of our ten-foot by twenty-foot cell. It was a cone of all our crap, clothing, bedding, toiletries, and stationery. My eleven dorm mates and I let out a groan as we went to disassemble the pile looking for our pathetic items. I grabbed the first blanket I came across and wrapped up with my arms folded over my chest while I watched the others pick through the mess. We didn't get far before the call came, "standing head count! Inmates by your bunks!"

When this round of blundered head counting was finished, and the jumbled pile of our belongings had been sorted, I curled up in my bunk wearing what was surely a pair of someone else's underpants, while my wet clothing hung over the bottom rail of my bunk to drip.

This chapter could have also been titled "The best things in life are free." My wife and I have the most fun hiking, playing cards, or having barbecues with our friends and kids. Building memories and storing them in our hearts can't be beat!

Clearly, things could always be worse. These types of events played out time and time again throughout my years of incarceration, though none quite as bone chillingly cold. My possessions were ransacked, broken, or confiscated many times, and I had to learn to find happiness and contentment within myself, because it was the only thing that could not be taken away. At least the underpants were dry.

Chapter Thirteen

NEVER JUDGE A BOOK BY ITS COVER

A FEW MONTHS INTO my bid at Fort Dix I was assigned a job in the carpentry department. Starting pay was 4 cents an hour, much better than the 2 cents I would have been getting had I been given an orderly job, sweeping hallways in the cell block.

My compadres and I would tackle everything from repairing doors or stairs in different parts of the prison, to replacing a roof over the visiting center.

It always amazes me when I meet people who are surprised to learn that inmates get paid to work in the prison they're housed. The American taxpayer could never foot the bill for all the workers it would take to keep a prison running. Electricians, plumbers, HVAC crews, food service workers, painters, carpenters, the list goes on and on. The few dollars inmates get to work allows them to buy stamps, make phone calls, and keep themselves supplied with toiletries and basic necessities. Not to mention idle hands are the tools of the devil and all that. Trust me, prisoners are up to plenty of shenanigans with the little free time they have left after work; there'd be complete chaos otherwise.

The tools we used were kept under a tight watch. You can imagine how it would look if they'd forgotten to inventory a pair of bolt cutters at the end of the day, that would make for an embarrassing headline. "700 Inmates escape using bolt cutters." Not to mention, a screwdriver makes one hell of a shank!

Now believe it or not, an inmate is placed in charge of distributing and collecting tools to and from the other inmates each day. Of course, a CO checks the inventory before anyone is allowed to leave, but talk about having the mice watch over the cheese! Anyways, I was given the job of crib attendant. The guy responsible for distributing and collecting the tools each day. I would take inmate-assigned tags in exchange for tools they needed. Mostly I would spend my time reading, writing, or drawing while listening to my radio with earbuds, usually Howard Stern. He could still be heard on terrestrial ratio back then.

We had a great group of guys in that shop. Some were really skilled carpenters, and some guys just landed the job by luck, but either way we all got along and usually had a good time passing the days. When there wasn't work to be done, we'd spend our time playing cards or swapping war stories. We had everyone from two-bit hustlers to druggies to bigwigs in the financial world. People who never would have met had it not been for the circumstances that brought us there.

It was that comradery that led to me dropping my guard and forgetting the fact that I was in prison and living by a different set of rules than those of the outside world. It was a rainy day, and everyone was just milling about either playing cards or working on little craft projects the head screw was allowing us to work on. I was in the tool crib, my usual home for the workday. I stepped out of my crib to use the john, and when I returned, I noticed that one of my coworkers, David, had taken a DeWalt screw gun from my area. "I need your tag, David," I said in a congenial tone as I closed the bottom of the Dutch door to my room behind me. "Mind your business, tool man," came his reply. I stood a little dumbfounded looking at the back of his head, not sure I'd really heard him right. David and I got along rather well and were a great team at playing pinochle. Plus, he was a slight little guy, maybe one hundred and fifty pounds soaking wet standing five foot five. I was a two-hundred and fifty-five-pound dude and although it was mostly fat, the balls on this kid shocked me. He walked to my right without looking back, and out of my view from my place in the crib. I saw the screw gun sitting in the table where he'd been working and decided to just step out and retrieve it. I'd only gotten a few steps towards the work bench before I felt the first blow coming from my blind side, right in the face. I staggered back a few steps while trying to gain my wits and raise my fists. I turned to face my attacker David, but only got a glimpse of him before he taunted, "Oh, you want some more, tool man?" and blasted me with several more shots. I felt my eyes water and blood squirt from my nose. I must have landed at least one blow—probably to his skull—because I could tell I'd broken a knuckle on my right index finger. I heard myself ask in a pathetic voice, "What the fuck, dude, why are you hitting me?" Not one of my prouder moments. His only response came in the form of flying fists. He hit me so many times with a right, I was begging for a left. Before long, I felt my world tilt and I fell to the ground. I'd hoped that would be the end of it, and I even heard the guys in the room telling him I'd had enough, but he began stomping me and kicking me in the ribs with those steel-toed work boots. I rolled and rolled to avoid the kicks but soon found myself wedged against a workbench. My vision cleared long enough to catch sight of him winding up to kick me dead in the face. Just then he was swarmed by a group of guys who pulled him away from me and they ushered him out the front door.

I struggled to my hands and knees and watched as a pool of blood formed on the floor and quickly grew to the size of a dinner plate. Someone handed me a ball of paper towels and when I pressed it to my face, my nose felt like a bag of Legos. I made my way on wobbly legs to the bathroom. The shop orderly was already mopping the blood, and he followed me as I went, cleaning the trail I left behind.

I was mortified when I looked at myself in the polished sheet of stainless steel that served as a mirror. My nose was completely folded over to one side, my eye socket was caved in, and my left cheek was swollen to the size of an orange. Rocky looked better after Apollo Creed was finished with him! I couldn't believe it—that tiny man had pulverized me! His wrists were no bigger than two of my fingers held together. I thought we were cool, if not friends, so why?

Pretty soon guys were coming to tell me that they had gotten David out at the last gate unlock and now I had to come up with a story as to why I looked the way I did. Welcome to life in the inside. A place where you get the shit kicked out of you, and it's your job to protect the asshole who did it to you! I pulled the paper towels away from my face and looked at the group, "You tell me how the fuck I can explain this!" They all cringed, then shrugged. "I'll do what I need to do," I said, meaning I'd make up some ridiculous story that wouldn't be believed and wind up in the SHU for my efforts. And that's exactly what happened. I said I fell on my face; they didn't believe me. They interrogated me for hours with no medical attention other than an ice pack. They didn't even attempt to straighten my nose, it being cosmetic and all that. I spent the next three months in the SHU healing from my wounds and being punished for not telling on my assailant. David, of course, was found out after a line up was conducted and he couldn't hide the wounds on his hands. He was shipped off to another prison yard that was segregated while I was in the hole. The orderly who mopped up all the blood got a few months in the SHU as well for destroying evidence.

To top it all off, when I finally returned to the general population, I was shunned for the first few weeks by everyone on the compound. It was assumed that I'd ratted on David. The wounds on David's knuckles hadn't been enough logic to convince the masses that he'd been caught by detection, it took a letter from David himself to release me from suspicion. In the letter he'd sent to one of his buddies he'd explained that he'd not been taking his psych meds for weeks and I had just been in the wrong place at the wrong time. No hard feelings on his part. *Gee thanks!* Also, he confirmed that when his knuckles gave him away during the lineup, he confessed to attacking me. I returned the favor by not pressing charges, and believe me, it was a favor to both of us. Being labeled a rat makes you a marked man. Life on the inside for a rat is about the same as that of a child molester. You're not only shunned, unable interact with any but the other dregs of society, but a constant target for anyone looking to take out some aggression for no reason at all. It's like a prison inside of prison. So, thanks again David, you did the right thing in the end.

You never know what someone else is going through at any given moment in time. This is especially true now as the global Covid-19 pandemic is disrupting our lives to varying degrees. I have to stop and remind myself often to be kinder and more patient with others even when they seem not to deserve it. Anyone one of us could be David—a powder keg ready to explode.

Chapter Fourteen

NECESSITY IS THE MOTHER OF INVENTION

I'VE SEEN SOME INGENIOUS devices constructed from the most rudimentary supplies one could imagine. Real MacGyver type stuff.

I've already told you about how to make fire using a pencil, some tissue paper, and a wall socket, but at Fort Dix a fella there was making pocket lighters he'd sell for about ten bucks if I remember correctly.

These devices used two AA batteries, some electrical tape, a piece of steel wool, a small piece of cardboard and a little piece of foil from a cigarette pack. The batteries were taped together, a negative and positive end at each end. A single strand of steel wool was taped across the leads of one end. A cardboard lid was fashioned to protect that end when in your pocket, and on the outside of the lid was taped a piece of foil.

When you needed a light, you removed the lid and pressed the foil to the bottom of the batteries, energizing the circuit. The steel wool would glow red hot from the resistance in a moment or two and just like that, you were lighting a smoke.

Another trick that was devised to fill a need was that of an engraver. Wherever you bought an am/FM radio from the commissary, they would engrave your ID number on it. If you were caught with a radio that did not have your ID number on it, they assume you stole it, or won it gambling and would confiscate it. So, if you wanted to sell or trade your radio, you would use a nail file to sand smooth the original ID number. Then use a thumb tack, heated with a cigarette cherry to do a makeshift engraving of the new number you wanted on the radio.

Some inventions were more important than others. I had a celly one time who was in imminent danger of being attacked—for what I don't recall—but the threat was real. My celly, Phil, spent about two weeks manufacturing a shank out of tissue paper and toothpaste. I don't know if it was the prison-issue toothpaste that was the key to this project or not, but it would harden into a cement-like glue. Phil spread a thin layer of the paste onto the tissue paper, then rolled it into a cone. He would only do a few layers a day. "Better to let the thing dry and harden," he told me. At the end of the two weeks, he had created a serviceable shank that would only be good for only one use before it would break. "It won't go through clothing, so I'll have to aim for the neck," Phil told me and made a stabbing motion to his own neck for a visual.

Phil hadn't gone to the yard since learning of the threat, but now that he had something to defend himself with, he was ready. He stuffed the inside of his shirt with magazines to help repel any body shots from a real shank, tucked his weapon into his sleeve and headed off to his fate on the yard. It didn't go well for him. He was jumped by a group of guys, never having had a chance to deploy his weapon. He was hauled off in an ambulance and I never learned of the outcome.

Stingers are a popular item of invention. These are tools created from some type of metal with an electrical cord attached to it. You plug it in the wall, and you can use it to boil water for all your jailhouse culinary needs. I don't know what kind of metal is used, or where in the hell it comes from, but you'd be surprised at the availability of things on the prison compound.

Once I saw the Cadillac of stingers. It was really a variation of the idea, and it was dubbed the George Foreman grill. Some genius used a hotel pan that was stolen from the kitchen and turned it into a grill. I found it in use in the cell of a well-known mobster in residence at Fort Dix. This guy was a character. If you've watched any true crime mob documentaries, I'm sure you'd recognize the name, but I'll just call him Anthony. I was with a pal who needed to see Anthony, and we opened the door to his cell and were hit with a wafting of smoke and fragrance of grilling food, just like at a diner. I couldn't believe it; they were grilling chicken breasts, Philly cheesesteak sandwiches, and garlic bread all at the same time on this thing. "Hey, shut the door youse guys, we don't need the fuzz catching wind of this, capiche?" Anthony gently scolded us upon entering.

He eventually had it taken away by the screw on duty one night. Anthony had the balls to confront the unit counselor when he came to work the next morning (in front of everyone). "Hey, dis fucking guy took my property. I need you to get it back for me." The counselor just shook his head and he continued on into the building, knowing what kind of day he would be having.

Tattoo guns could be made from any kind of motor. They used to sell Walkman cassette players back in the day, and some of the components from those survived through the years. You could buy both battery-operated and 110-volt fans in the commissary to combat the summer heat. Those motors were bulkier, but could be used for tattooing.

A cringe-worthy artifact I saw one time was a syringe. You have to be dedicated to your addiction to use the device I saw, but if you're detoxing from heroin, you'll do just about anything!

This thing was manufactured using an eye dropper that had a needle secured to the end of it. The needle was extracted from the innards of an incandescent light bulb. The handy emery board was used to sharpen the end of the needle. I asked a guy that I knew had used the thing what it felt like. "Like jabbing a rusty nail into your vein, but it gets the job done," he told me.

Some of these guys could have been engineers had they put their skills and energy into it. The inventiveness and perseverance of people can surprise you. I wonder what sort of things prisoners during the Holocaust did to make life a little more bearable during those dark times. Surely, they had less to work with than we did, but I'll bet they had something.

Chapter Fifteen

DISCRETION IS THE BETTER PART OF VALOR

"Inmate Gilford, report to the CO's office," came the call over the PA in a sweet female voice. I was reading on my bunk when my eleven other cellmates immediately began hooting and hollering,

"Oh snap, you're getting some tonight."

"Gilford's taking a trip to poon town."

CO Shaw had a reputation for being "friendly" with the inmates since long before I arrived at FCI, Fort Dix, NJ.

It didn't happen every night she was on duty, but her M.O. was to call an inmate to her office for a "random" breathalyzer. Once there, she'd have the inmate close the door behind them, and Bob's your uncle so to speak. Now, being alone with any CO behind closed doors is a big no-no, and especially with a female CO, and yet it happened on a frequent basis.

CO Shaw was not an attractive woman by any stretch of the imagination. She was very short and what I would call morbidly obese. She had a face that could make a train take a dirt road, but she did have a voice as smooth as silk, and a pool of sex-starved inmates to choose from. Before I actually heard my name over the PA, I will admit I had thought about what I might do should I be selected by CO Shaw and may have even engaged in some shit-talking with the boys on the subject. However, once I began the long walk from my cell to her office three floors below, I felt my resolve crumbling. *I have less than two years remaining on my sentence. Then again, this had been going on for years without anyone getting caught. Of course, if anyone would get caught, it would be me.* The internal struggle continued as I walked, guys slapping me on the back and shouting words of encouragement or jealousy the entire way.

I arrived at the open door to her office and knocked on the door jamb. "Inmate Gilford," I announced, my voice cracking as I spoke. She was seated at her desk, eyes fixed on the computer screen in front of her. "Come in," she ordered, not looking up. She let me walk the four steps it took to get to her desk before she told me, "Shut the door behind you." Her eyes stayed glued to her computer screen while I paused a moment to gather my thoughts before turning and making the short trek back to slowly close the door. The click it made as I closed the door seemed deafening to me but was probably no more than a barely audible metallic snap. I was in turmoil as I spun to walk back to her desk.

I stood there, palms sweating, CO Shaw lazily stared at her computer screen. I was struggling to come up with something to say when she let me off the hook by slowly turning her chair towards me. Her eyes remained on the screen for a half a beat, then looked up at me and held my gaze. My mind was racing. I thought about the fact that I'd been through a lot during my time on the inside. I've faced death on more than one occasion, and yet the prospect of getting laid had me scared shitless! I knew the right thing to do, but the mechanics of it were beyond me. She relieved me of my anguish when she opened a drawer in her desk and pulled out a breathalyzer and placed it on top of her desk. I glanced at the device, which looked like an old Walkman cassette player with a tube sticking out of the top.

"You know what I want you to do with this?" She asked.

"You want me to blow in that, right?" I replied. She nodded once, and I reached for the device. She held it fast as I tried to lift it to my lips.

"Can I hold it?"

"Let's hold it together," she said.

As I pulled the mechanism up, she only let it come off the desk a fraction of an inch before maneuvering it over to her leg, where she placed it upon her knee. Both our hands remained fixed on the device, and I considered letting go, but something kept my hand wrapped around it.

"Blow until you hear three beeps," she said. I made a feeble attempt at raising the breathalyzer again before relenting and getting on my knees to blow in the tube. I blew for what seemed an eternity. When the three beeps came, I gathered myself to rise up when she asked, "Anything else you want to put your lips on while you're down there?" I looked up to meet her eyes. She nodded towards her crotch with a wry smile, and I stuttered my response, "I-I-I'm g-g-gay, Ms. Shaw."

We stared at each other for a long couple of moments before she let me off the hook. "Too bad," she sighed before turning back to her desk with the breathalyzer in hand. "Leave the door open on your way out, Gilford," she told me as she went back to looking at her monitor. I'm sure she knew I was lying, but it allowed her to save face, sparing me from any possible repercussions.

I'd barely made it out the door before I heard the next man being paged over the PA: "Inmate Holcomb, report to the CO's office."

I was about halfway up the stairwell when I encountered Holcomb on his way down. He had a George Jefferson swagger and a shit-eating grin, "Couldn't get the job done, huh Gilford?"

"She needed more than I could give her, buddy," I replied.

I'd been back on my bunk for several minutes trying to get back into my book, amongst the ribbing my cellmates were giving me for my swift return when we heard the alarm sound.

It wasn't long before we learned that CO Shaw inadvertently hit the panic button while the two were going at it. Of course, she claimed he attacked her, and poor Holcomb found himself facing rape charges in addition to whatever he was already in for.

I wrote in my journal that night on how I'd narrowly escaped a horrific outcome. Discretion is the better part of valor. This was a defining moment in my life. One where I was finally able to forego some instant gratification, saving me from a lot of woe. I had always been a slave to that mindset, whether for drugs, sex, money, or whatever I desired. Mine was a classic case of the angel and devil sitting upon each shoulder, counseling me on the merits and risks of things I was considering. The angel finally made a good enough case for me to listen!

Chapter Sixteen
BUNS OF STEEL

IT'S A TRICKY THING, the relationship between inmates and screws. You want to be a good worker, and not get caught doing stupid shit that would cause any grief for the CO's you work for. Also, you want to be in a good enough position to ask for a favor, (like getting your buddy a job), but you don't want to seem so cozy that you're labeled a rat, or a cop lover. Luckily for me, my friend Bob had been in just such a position.

Bob and I met back in county jail while we were awaiting transfer. He was a white-collar criminal, doing time for some sort of Ponzi scheme, while I had been busted for manufacturing methamphetamine. We lived in completely different worlds, and would never have met out on the streets, let alone become friends, but prison is a great equalizer.

Bob had managed to get me a job in the wellness department sometime after I'd been released from the SHU when David had kicked the shit out of me. My job in the carpentry department had been filled by someone else. Just as well, I had bad memories of that place anyways.

I began my tenure as a clerk, where I would do things like schedule fitness classes, make flyers for upcoming events, and post them around the compound and in each cell block. The wellness department was a great place to work. It was located on the third floor of a converted cell block that now housed both a law library and a reading library on the first floor, classrooms on the second floor, and the wellness and hobby craft departments on the third floor. My job allowed me time during the day to take various classes downstairs and to use the computer lab to make my flyers and signup sheets.

I shared the clerk's office with a Korean guy named Kim who was the head clerk and fitness instructor. This guy was jacked! Kim was only 5'7" but built like an Asian hulk. His long black ponytail gave him the look of a samurai, but his sense of humor softened the effect of his imposing looks. He was in his mid-forties when I first met him, and he proved to be one of the most genuine, smart, and caring men I have ever known. He'd been in the United States since he was eighteen years old, but his thick Korean accent never left him. He loved to call everyone "shorty," which should have been a derogatory term being that "shorty" was used to describe girls by most of the inmate population. Nobody ever seemed to take offense when Kim called them shorty, however. We all took it for the good-natured jab as it was intended, coming from a short man. He loved to jokingly accuse everyone of being racist, too. Like one time there was a group of us hanging out in the clerk's office and we were trying to solve a particularly difficult math problem while Kim sat with his feet upon the desk reading a book. Eventually I asked, "Hey Kim, can you help us with this problem?"

He brought his feet down, sat up and closed his book and replied, "Yo shorty, you think just because I'm Asian that I'm good at math or something? You fucking racist! Next you probably say something about how I'm no good at driving the car!" I was used to this by now from Kim, so I was ready with a comeback.

"Well let me ask you this, Kim: How many cars have you owned?"

"Four," came the reply.

"Okay, how many have you crashed?"

Kim started laughing as he spoke the word, "four."

Once our laughter subsided, I asked, "So what's the answer then?" sliding the paper with the problem to him. It took him all of two seconds to come up with the answer, "It's thirty-seven, you stupid bastards!"

It was with Kim's prodding that I eventually started to add physical fitness to the things I'd spend my time working on during my five-year stay at Club Fed. He'd say to me, "Yo, Danger, when you gonna do something about that belly, you fat bastard?" At first, I'd reply with something like, "I'm the fitness clerk, not the fitness instructor." However, it had been becoming apparent to me that a lot of guys were coming through those doors as fat bastards, and slowly but surely changing their bodies for the better. When I looked down at my enormous belly, or stepped on the scale, which at the time read over two hundred and sixty pounds, I did yearn to be fit. I just didn't want to put in the effort. I mean, I couldn't tie my shoes without coming up for a breath of air halfway through each shoe, so something had to be done.

Under Bob and Kim's tutelage I began a fitness regimen that was rather pathetic at first. The boys knew what they were doing when they told me for the first week, I would only do five minutes on the stair master on the lowest setting each day. I argued at first that I could do much more, and that five minutes wouldn't get me anywhere, but eventually relented and agreed to follow their advice. Good thing I did, as I found those five minutes to be all my overweight body and smoker's lungs could handle!

It was a long haul before I was able to do even twenty minutes straight on the machine. Eventually, though, I started to see some results on the scale. "Down five pounds!" I proclaimed enthusiastically one day as I stepped off the scale that was located just outside the door to the clerk's office. Kim was behind his desk and his celly Eric was in a chair in front of his desk. "Congratulations, Danger, only four hundred and fifty to go," Eric quipped.

"Yo shorty, you one to talk, you fat bastard. At least Danger is doing something about it, you just sitting there getting fatter every day!" Kim snapped before laughing at his own joke. Eric was a chubby, short little guy with a bald head. He sort of had an Uncle Fester thing going on, but he was a good dude. "Yo, Danger, you doing good man, but let me ask you about your diet. What you eating?" Kim asked in that thick accent of his. "The same shit we all eat. It's not like I can run to the health food store and pick something up. Whatever they serve, that's what I eat," I explained. "Yeah, but you don't have to eat everything they put in front of you. You know that, right?" He went on to quiz me about each and everything I put into my mouth over the course of a normal day and made suggestions on things I could alter or omit from my diet. Turns out a glazed honey bun right before bed each night was counterproductive to my physical fitness! Who knew?

I couldn't fathom making all the changes Kim was recommending I make at first, but his advice was taking root and I made my first concession soon after, which was to switch from whole milk to 2% skim. Next was cutting out soda, and eventually bread and then the sugar in my coffee. Each change was painful at first, and there would generally be a month or two between each change before I could muster up the courage to do more.

After six months or so, I'd gotten my weight down about twenty pounds and my trainers Kim and Bob decided that I was serious enough and had enough commitment to allow me into the gym with them to lift some weights. This was a great honor because getting into the gym was easy, but there was fierce completion for access to the actual weights. People would monopolize them, and some guys were actually paid to get there early and hold the weights and benches until their benefactors arrived. Kim always got what he wanted whenever he went in, and I assumed that he paid for the privilege. Turns out he was just so respected that guys made way for him.

Once I started lifting weights, the results came faster. Where it had taken me six long months to lose my first twenty pounds, it only took me another two months to lose the next twenty! I was down to about two hundred and twenty pounds and feeling fantastic. It was at this time that Kim hit me with a shocker.

We were having a meeting in the office with all the fitness instructors. Kim was seated behind his desk leaning back in his chair, his fingers formed into a steeple, which he was tapping gently against his lips in a manner of thoughtful contemplation. I was seated at my own desk with a notepad and pen at the ready. Jose, our basic aerobics instructor, was seated in a chair directly in front of my desk with the chair turned sideways so he could rest his arm on my desktop while he drummed his fingers in boredom. Raqib, the circuit training guru, was seated in front of Kim's desk leaning forward in his chair with his hands on his knees looking intently at Kim. Raqib had proposed a new class he'd like to teach called "total body sculpting" and was anxious to hear whether Kim was going to allow it. Bob, who taught the senior circuit class, was reclined in a chair against the back wall, lazily thumbing through a newspaper. Our last remaining instructor was Doc, a former paramedic who headed up the abs class, and he was leaning up against a wall to Bob's left, looking over his shoulder to peep at the paper.

Kim's fingers unraveled, then pointed at Jose. "You going to teach circuit training next quarter." Jose nodded in agreement. "Raqib, you can do your class, but you also have to take over my advanced aerobics this quarter. I'm not gonna teach a class this time." Raqib mouthed the word *yes* and gave a slow motion first pump in the air. "Bob and Doc, you guys do same class as this quarter. Danger," Kim paused while I perked up to look at him. "You gonna teach basic aerobics this time." I was floored. "Me? I've never even attended a class, let alone teach one!" I argued. "There two classes left this quarter, you go into Jose's class to get the idea. You be fine, it's nothing but fat bastards anyways. You know, your people, shorty," Kim chuckled as he said these last few words. I wrote my name on the pad with the words "basic aerobics" next to it and just stared for a moment, letting the fear take root in my stomach. Basic aerobics was all calisthenics and was an hour long! I was doing great with my personal fitness, but *one hour*?

The next night I attended Jose's class and paid careful attention to all the exercises he was performing. I made mental notes of the things I thought he did well, like giving us a chance to recover a little by having everyone line up in rows of four and having one group of people do lunges across the room and back before the next group would go. He also did some things I thought I should avoid when I taught the class like using the same muscle groups for two consecutive exercises like pushups followed by burpees. The good news is that I was able to perform all the exercises during the two classes of Jose's that I attended. I just wasn't sure I'd be able to give instructions while doing them with all the gasping for air I was doing!

We had a two-week period between classes each quarter to get people signed up and do equipment maintenance, so that gave me time each day to go into the workout room and develop my routine. I was nervous, but by the night that my first class came around, I felt I was as prepared as I could be, given the circumstances. I sat at my desk watching the clock. Kim and some fellas were hanging out chatting about whatever the topic of the evening was, while I tried to follow the conversation. I'd decided early on to hide my fears and nervousness from the boys. Kim was not going to change his mind about me teaching the class, and I was not going to give them any fodder for ball breaking, our favorite pastime.

My appointed time arrived, and I found myself walking down the hall to the exercise room feeling like I was hovering above my body, watching myself below. I entered the room and made myself busy setting out the steps for the step aerobics portion of the class I would be starting with. I placed twenty steps in neat rows throughout the room, plus the one I'd use at the head of the class where I would face the men. I took my position behind my step and welcomed everyone as they entered the room. I noticed the clock on the wall at the far end of the room said two minutes to start time, and I felt my bowels instantly turn to liquid. I had to clench my ass cheeks together in panic as I waddled across the hall to the restrooms. What transpired there was volcanic in nature, to use a euphemism, and left me feeling weak and nauseated. I returned to the room just in time to see that big hand of the clock strike seven thirty. I spoke to the group in a voice loud, clear, and full of confidence (you know, faking it completely), "Okay guys, everyone line up behind your steps." And just like that, my trial by fire had begun. I was off to a fairly good start, everyone was pretty much keeping pace with me, and I could tell by the perspiration on the foreheads and open-mouthed breathing that I was able to set a challenging tempo for the group.

About fifteen minutes into the routine had passed when I noticed Kim, Eric and Jose crowding at the skinny vertical window of the door to gawk at me and my performance. I tried to ignore their mocking faces and to concentrate on my rhythm. Eventually they were too great of a distraction, so I moved the men to a planking and crunches series of exercises so I would be forced to face away from the window. It broke the distraction for me, and I was able to finish the class without giving them a second thought.

I dismissed the class and was pleased when I received praise and thanks from most everyone in the room. Some guys came up to give me a fist bump and to tell me about the parts of the class they felt were especially good, or difficult. As the men filed out of the room, I glimpsed Kim and Eric loitering in the hall outside the door, but just then the last participant who'd been hanging back in the room approached me. "Danger, that class was so amazing," he began in flamboyant, New York accent. "I really felt challenged, and every time I thought I was just about to collapse, you'd switch to a new exercise, and I was able to keep going. It was super great." His voice was gruff and gravelly like that of Harvey Firestein. I thanked him for his kind words and skillfully extracted myself from the conversation quickly before I was caught alone in a room with a homosexual man who may or may not have been hitting on me. Thankfully, Kim and Eric were no longer outside the door when I began to make my way back to the office. *Dodged a bullet there*, I thought.

I strode down the hall towards the office full of pride and a sense of achievement. I didn't think I had it in me, but once Kim put me under the gun, I'd risen to the challenge. I was grateful to Kim for what he'd done for me. Nothing could bring me down.

I entered the office to find Kim, Eric and Doc red faced and giggling at what seemed to be a hilarious inside joke. "What's so funny, guys?" I asked innocently. Eric answered in a very passable Harvey Firestein impersonation, "I don't know what you're talking about, Danger, we were just talking about how great your class was. I think we should change the name to 'Buns of Steel'!" I instantly felt my elation depleting, and I knew that this was not something that was likely to end well or soon!

The "buns of steel" references were relentless over the next two days leading up to my next class. Eric remade my basic aerobics flyers with the "Buns of Steel" name and cartoon people sticking their butts out. He posted them around the wellness department. Thankfully, the CO in charge kept him from putting them up in the dorms, but he was good humored enough to allow them up in our building. *Thanks, dude!*

There was about an hour and a half between dinner and my class during which I had to endure the fellas tormenting me in the office. "Yo, Danger," Kim began "How about we see if we can pump in some music to your room for the class? What songs would you like?"

"How about Stand by your Man," Doc offered.

"I'm Too Sexy for my Shirt," Kim added.

"I know, how about It's Raining Men!" Eric exclaimed. The group had a good laugh at that one. I wanted to show that their teasing wasn't getting to me, but I couldn't think of a song title, so I chimed in with "How about I skip the class and just show the movie Brokeback Mountain?" My response had the desired effect: everyone laughed, fooling them into thinking I was unfazed by their antics. To quote a sportswriter I'm fond of, "If you ever find yourself being drummed out of town, pick up a baton and act like you're leading the parade!"

I entered my room that night to find that my class had grown from twenty to thirty participants, and all the new members seemed to be friends of my Mr. Firestein. Turns out his name was actually Lorenzo. I looked up to find the usual faces crowding the window in the door, cracking up at my misfortune.

There was nothing I could do but to start the class. So, I did. At the end, after all the "straight folks" had left, Lorenzo and his gang of flamboyant friends approached me to tell me how much they loved the class. I was a little uneasy, to say the least, to be the subject of their admiration. On the streets it wouldn't have bothered me in the least. In fact, I think I'd be flattered. However, there were different rules at play in the place we were residing, and I couldn't think of a way out of my situation.

Lorenzo spoke for the group when he said, "Danger, we loved the class! We were wondering if you'd be willing to help us with setting up workouts that we could do on the days that we don't have class. And maybe with our diets too? We'd pay you, of course."

And just like that, I was now in the business of selling fitness plans, and it paid well. I especially found it humorous when those of Spanish-speaking heritage approached me, having heard that my nickname was "Danger," and not knowing that it was a tongue in cheek sort of thing, would approach me sheepishly to ask if they could purchase my services. "Excuse me, uh, Mr. Danger?" Or my favorite: "El Peligro sir"

Kim eloquently pointed out that I catered to the "fat bastard" segment of the population, and it was true. It worked well because they'd all seen me slowly transform from a fat bastard to a somewhat slimmer bastard, and that gave them hope. I was one of them, and I was doing it. It's hard to take fitness advice from some Greek god who's been born with great genetics.

I don't think I had to go to the commissary myself for the next three months. I would just give the guys my shopping lists, and my orders would appear at my cell just like Amazon!

I still caught flak from the boys in the office, but it was a lot easier to take once I had monetized the situation. The trick was customizing each plan, so they didn't just all share the same plan. I found ways to do just that and when they achieved success, word of mouth brought me even more customers.

I learned that it doesn't pay to discriminate. I was extremely uncomfortable with Lorenzo's sexual orientation because of the trouble it could cause me. However, since I didn't dismiss him and his friends outright because of it, I wound up profiting nicely from the association. Also, a more valuable thing I gained was integrity and respect. Although at first, I was the butt of jokes from the fellas in the office, in the end they saw not only my entrepreneurship, but also my conviction to not be swayed by public opinion or pressure. I stuck with those guys and helped most of them make significant strides in their fitness goals, and I was immensely proud of that.

I learned the value of hustling. I had a job that paid 12 cents an hour as a clerk in the wellness department, which covered all my monthly needs like toiletries and postage stamps, and that's all I really needed. However, with this new stream of income I was able to start saving money. I'd never saved a dime in my life up to that point! Plus, I was able to buy healthier foods from the commissary like tuna fish, which helped me to build muscle and lose weight. Soon after, thanks to Kim, I had another hustle helping guys with their course work in becoming personal fitness trainers. I even became certified myself in the process (though I never used it once I was released). Also, since I had a typewriter at my desk in the clerk's office, I helped guys by typing legal papers like appeals and whatnot, which generated even more money. I even added typing up gambling slips for bookies on my handy typewriter, a gig that paid very well. All of these things together helped me to leave prison with enough money to get on my feet before I even had a job. Which was something I desperately needed, being that I had absolutely nothing to start with.

All this taught me that I was capable of more than I thought I was. I never would have thought I could handle instructing that class. Without Kim's prodding I never would have tried. Thankfully, I've been able to push myself through scary situations where I wondered if I could handle them, and since then I've had good success. Sometimes things are pushed onto me as well, but I have this experience to bolster my confidence and I've achieved much in my life I may not have, had it not been for this pivotal experience.

Chapter Seventeen

ALWAYS BE PREPARED

Instructors in the Wellness department would occasionally give lectures on health and nutrition in the drug rehabilitation unit. As I progressed on my journey to better health and nutrition while working in the wellness department, Kim decided that I should start shadowing one of our instructors who gave these lectures. First, I began with another fella named Kevin who taught nutrition courses. I would sit beside him at the head of the class twice a week and take notes just as I had done while studying Jose as he taught the basic aerobics class. Once again, I took notice of the parts I thought worked well, and of the things I thought could be done better, or that were missing all together. Between the things I'd learned while studying for the personal trainer certification course, and what I picked up from Kevin in the classes, I felt I was getting a well-rounded education.

Once a quarter, one of our instructors would give a talk to the substance abuse education program. Doc had been filling this role for the past couple of years, but being that he was coming up for release, once again Kim determined that it was I who should be groomed to replace him. Fun side note: Doc hated my guts. For what, I'm not exactly sure, but it was probably my closeness to Kim. It was clear that Kim liked me and took an interest in advancing my personal development. This irked a lot of guys who wanted to be part of Kim's inner circle.

Kim was always referring people to me for all kinds of hustles, like helping with the fitness courses, typing up gambling slips for bookies, and typing legal documents for those who were filing court appeals and other documents. Kim never took a kick back on all that business he sent my way either, though I always offered.

So, it was no surprise to me that when Doc was informed of my apprenticeship, his face pulled a scowl. Doc told me to forget everything I thought I knew, and to just watch, listen, and learn while he gave the lectures. I humbled myself and agreed, knowing that it would only be a short time I had to endure this uncomfortable arrangement.

We had been scheduled to give the first class on a morning at 7:30 am. This gave everyone in the prison time to eat breakfast and get to wherever they had to be before the 7:00 am closure of the compound, which stopped all movement of inmates between buildings. I arrived in plenty of time and waited outside the classroom. I passed the time listening to a morning radio program on my portable AM/FM player without a care in the world. That is until it got dangerously close to seven. The woman who taught the class, came into the hallway, and asked if we were all set. "Well, Doc isn't here yet, so...." I began. She cut me off with a reassuring, "That's okay, I'm sure you can handle it if he doesn't show." She then turned and returned to the classroom. Panic sank into my guts as I realized I'd missed my chance to tell her no, I was not prepared to deliver the lecture. Next came the familiar announcement over the PA, "Attention on the compound and in the housing units: recall, recall, recall. The compound is now closed, all inmates return to your housing units or to your work details. Recall, recall, recall." My heart sank. I was unprepared, I had no notes, no plan, and what's worse, my mind went blank to all the things I had learned over the past year and a half. All the studying, the note taking, the essays I'd written, and even all the things I'd done to transform my body to the state it was in at that time, just evaporated from my mind. Foolishly I decided to just cowboy up and go in that class and wing it.

It went about as bad as you could imagine. I found myself before that class stammering and repeating myself two and three times over. I could feel the familiar cold sweat soaking through my underarms and washing down my lower back as it always did when I became nervous or stressed out. I could see from the looks on the faces of those in attendance that it was nearly as painful for those watching me bomb as it was to be bombing. I eventually hit a bit of a stride near the end of the class once I started taking questions, but it was too little too late and everyone in the room knew it.

That night as I walked the hallway towards the office, I heard the boys yucking it up with merriment. I paused a few feet from the door and acted like I was tying my bootlace in case I was spotted so that I could eavesdrop on the conversation. I heard Kim's voice first, "Yo, Doc, just admit it, you left Danger hanging out to dry on purpose!" Doc's reply came in a tone that let everyone know his words were insincere. "Why no, Kim, I just didn't make the gate unlock in time." The room erupted in laughter again as the logistics of my betrayal were made plain for all to see. I picked this moment to make my entrance. As expected, the laughter immediately died down as the inhabitants of the room tried to seem as though nothing was amiss. Kim quickly snatched up a scrap of paper and studied it intently. Jorge began picking imaginary lint from his pants leg, and Doc, who had been leaning against the wall in front of Kim's desk made some excuse as to where he had to be and exited the room. Eric, who'd been sitting behind my desk when I arrived, got up to give me my seat. As he passed me, he asked with a shit eating grin, "How's it going, Danger?"

"Oh, you know," I replied as I looked over the fellas in the room. Eric was the only one making eye contact; he loved this sort of thing. Jose continued picking at his pants, not looking up. Kim was still engaged with his piece of paper, which I now saw was last week's menu from the cafeteria, and it was upside down. "How's it going with you, Kim?" I asked. He fought to control his smirk as he answered without looking up from his fascinating menu "Oh, you know."

I broached the subject on everyone's mind to cut the tension in the room. "Well, wanna hear about my day?" I asked. "

"Oh, we heard about your day, Danger!" Eric exclaimed, bringing renewed nervous laughter from the boys.

"What happened, Danger? You been studying all this stuff for months. You teaching classes, helping the guys with their PT courses, what gives?" Kim prodded me, giving up the guise as though nothing was amiss. "Dude, I don't know. Maybe it was because Doc told me to forget everything I thought I knew, and just listen the first time. I drew a blank when I got stuck teaching the class. Once the panic set in, I couldn't remember my own name, let alone any fitness facts," I explained. "That fucker set me up!" I told the room.

"Yeah, he did, but you took the bait. All you had to do was cancel the class," Kim explained what I already knew.

Two months later, another date was set for Doc and me to give another lecture. This time I was prepared. I wrote out an entire lesson plan that could take up more than the allotted hour, just in case. I had material on basic fitness and nutrition, like how to adjust your caloric intake based on fitness goals like losing weight or gaining muscle. I also had a segment on myths and misconceptions. I'd witnessed many a person over the course of my stay at Club Fed trying to lose weight by layering on clothes and even wearing trash bags with holes cut out for their head and arms to increase the amount they would sweat during a workout in an effort to lose weight—a total myth. In short, I was prepared. Or so I thought.

On the appointed day I was once again early to the class. I passed the time studying my notes and rehearsing how I'd phrase certain things in the event the day played out the same as they had before. To my surprise, Doc arrived on time. He even gave me a pleasant greeting, "Good morning, Danger. You ready to do this?" He asked as he headed into the classroom. I gave him a "yep" and followed behind him.

At the start of the class the teacher welcomed everyone, then introduced Doc and me as the day's speakers. Doc stood up at the head of the class while I remained seated in an empty desk off to the side. "Good morning guys," Doc began, "We're here to give you some basics on fitness and nutrition. My friend Mr. Gilford here, better known on the compound as "Danger," will kick us off with a broad overview, then I'll jump in at the end and give you some specifics on how to achieve particular fitness goals. Danger?" Doc smirked as he made a flourish with his arms towards me. *Here it is* I thought, *at least he had the balls to throw me under the bus in person this time!* I gathered my notes and took up position in front of the class. It went beautifully! My words came easy, my thoughts were expressed clearly and succinctly, and my manner was confident. I had been prepared this time, and I could tell from the gradual change in Doc's expression from smug to annoyed, that I was nailing it!

I could have gone on, but I wrapped up my segment with fifteen minutes left so that Doc could do his thing and hopefully salvage some modicum of peace between us. What happened next was astonishing. Doc began taking questions, and in his answers, systematically contradicted everything I had just taught. Where I had said that in order to feed muscle growth in tandem with heavy weightlifting, one would need to increase their protein intake from 15-20% of their caloric intake to 25-30%, Doc said that was a myth and that they'd need to eat mostly carbs. I'd told them that eating before bed would cause an increase in stored fat in the body, Doc told them that eating right before bed gave the body the energy it needed to do necessary repairs and would actually help to burn calories while they slept. It went on and on, but I just kept a straight face as if everything he said we're true and meshed perfectly with everything I'd said. Doc had an amazing physique, so I could understand the nodding heads and note taking from those in the class, but I cringed at the thought of people following his advice.

I need not have worried though. Soon enough after that painful day, Doc was released and only a month or so passed before I received a visit from a few of the fellas who had been in the class we taught together. Kim and I were sitting behind our desks in the wellness department when the motley crew appeared in the doorway. "Hello, Kim. Danger," the apparent spokesperson began. Kim always got the first hello out of respect, I noticed, even when he wasn't the person of interest in the situation.

"Hey Thomas, RJ, Shadow," Kim responded. (He always seemed to know everyone's name).

Thomas, the spokesman, continued, "We wanted to ask Danger about our workouts. We've been doing everything Doc told us we should be doing, and we don't seem to be making any progress"

"Progress?" Kim chimed in with surprise, "Yo, you guys look worse than before you started! Don't you remember anything Danger taught you in the class?" Thomas looked sheepish as he searched for a response. His two companions shuffled their feet and looked away in embarrassment. "Yo shorty, the class was free, but if you want Danger to help you now, you got to pay him, man. Thirty dollars each, and Danger get you where you need to be, okay?" And just like that, Kim had monetized the situation in my favor once again!

I wrote it in my journal, and it became sort of a mantra after that. Always be prepared. Life doesn't always go as planned. In fact, it often does not! In this case I had no excuse for not being prepared. I knew the information, and had I taken the time to organize some notes and rehearse, well, I wouldn't have had this story in the book. I owe Doc a debt of gratitude, however, because he did teach me some valuable lessons. I try to be prepared these days. If I'm going for a job interview, I research the company I'm applying to and practice my responses to typical questions interviewers like to throw at you. Some of my preparedness drives my wife a little nuts, like always filling my gas tank once it gets below half! Because you never know what could happen, and the New England winters can leave you stranded, and I like to have enough fuel to keep my heater going in case I slide off the road and have to wait for a tow truck.

The truth always comes out eventually. Right after that class I wanted to seek out all those who had been in attendance and try and repair the dikes, so to speak, I was embarrassed and wanted to set the record straight somehow. Kim advised I just let it go, and once again his counsel proved to be right. It proves to be much more satisfying once the truth comes out and people recognize that, than it does to convince someone you're right. I feel it shows more class and you'll be respected more for it in the end if they discover it on their own.

Chapter Eighteen

YOU NOT BUILT LIKE THAT, SHORTY

"You not built like that, ok shorty?" That phrase stung, I'm not gonna lie. I'd been getting ultra-fit (in my mind), in the months and years that followed since my association with Kim and the wellness department had begun. Between teaching aerobics classes, my morning workouts, and healthier eating habits, I'd really developed a solid fitness regimen. Along this journey I was also able to quit smoking. Every time I craved a cigarette, I would run some laps on the track, drop and do some pushups, or suck on a butterscotch candy, (only ten calories a piece). I'd gotten my weight down to 175 pounds, down a total of 85 pounds! I was able to do pull ups for the first time in my life! I was really stoked with my achievements.

Each day began at the crack of dawn when the PA system would crackle to life. "Attention in the housing units and on the compound, the gates are unlocked for chow time!" The guards took special delight in channeling Robin Williams' "Good morning Vietnam!" When they made this announcement, jarring us from our slumber. I would spring out of bed, dress quickly and head down two flights of stairs, out the front door of my cell block, and walk the quarter mile in the fresh—often frigid—open air to the chow hall. I'd cut out most of the crap they served there from my diet, but on a good day there would be some sort of egg dish. If it was French toast or cereal, I'd grab myself a cup of coffee and head back to my cell to make a small bowl of oatmeal with a scoop of peanut butter from my locker. Thanks to my fitness clients, I was in steady supply of commissary items that could supplement my meals when they served things that were counterproductive to my goals.

Open movement on the prison grounds was only allowed for a short time in the morning. This gave everyone time to eat and get to work or school. I didn't have to report to work until after lunch, so I used the first hour of the morning to run on the track, and then spend an hour in the weight room.

On this particular day I finally felt confident enough to wear my newly purchased tank top undershirt, also known as a wife beater. I'd always admired the guys who could pull off the wife beater look. Sure, some of them looked like real tools when they wore them to the Walmart, or out in public in general. There was a time and place for this brand of fashion, and prison seemed to be the perfect fit. I'd always had a massive spare tire (except when I was strung out on meth) so I'd always been self-conscious of my appearance wearing tight shirts of any kind. I usually avoided full length mirrors or catching a glimpse of my reflection in windows at all costs. But I was doing so well, I'd gotten some definition in the muscles of my arms, chest, and shoulders. My mid-section only had an inch of pinch, versus an entire fistful of blubber like when I started. Kim would tease me, "Yo shorty, when you gonna lose that pouch?" But I was proud of all the progress I'd made.

So, I arrived at the track this particular morning and stripped down to my jogging shorts and wife beater. It was hard at six o'clock in the morning to find a radio station that played music instead of the usual morning talk for commuters. I had to settle for a hip hop station instead of my preferred rock and roll, but the songs had some good beats to run to, so I embarked on my three-mile trek around the dirt oval. It felt good to be out running in the fresh morning air. I was feeling strong and felt like I was setting a good pace for myself. The shirt was stretched tight across my chest, and the cool air rushing under my arms kept me cool. I was feeling fantastic, at the height of my physical fitness! I finished in under 35 minutes, a new record for me. I credited the shirt for this achievement.

I left the track to shower and proceed with my day which likely included some sort of class they were offering at the time, lunch, and then work. I entered the office to find the usual afternoon gang hanging out in the office. Kim, Raqib, Eric and Doc. Jose was down the hall working on his salsa steps. He was due to be deported back to Costa Rica soon and wanted to be on point when it came to wooing the ladies.

We all exchanged hellos as I took my seat behind my desk. "Yo Danger, let me ask you something, okay?" Kim began the way he usually started a conversation. "Were you out on the track running in the wife beater today?"

"Yes, I was," came my proud reply as I waited for the compliments to come rushing in. I hadn't known I'd been spotted, but the fact that word had gotten back to Kim of how fit I was getting put a swell in my chest.

"Yo, you not built like that, ok shorty?" I was dumbstruck.

"What do you mean?"

He chuckled before he continued. "Yo man, you doing good, ok? But you not there yet, ok? You may think you look good, but you don't." I was crestfallen. Kim went on, oblivious to my turmoil and discontent, "Maybe if you ran with a life-sized poster of you before the weight loss, then people could appreciate your progress. But just running around in the wife beater? No, no, no, you not built like that, shorty!"

I reflected in my journal that night on how it was okay to have an accurate self-image and stay in your lane. You see people all the time out in public wearing something that isn't very flattering to their physique. They probably thought they could pull it off just like I had, but best to get a second opinion on these types of things.

Plus, having a bit of humility was not a bad thing. Not humiliation, which is what I initially felt upon Kim's speech to me. I was bragging about my achievements by wearing that wife beater on the track, and while I'd made great strides up to that point, I was in no condition to try and pull off the look I was going for. A painful reminder that no matter how far you've come, there's always room for improvement!

Chapter Nineteen

NEVER BITE THE HAND THAT FEEDS YOU

S HAMUS WAS AN I RISH prick who showed up on the compound one day. He was loud and obnoxious, and constantly worked the plight of the Irish under English tyranny into every conversation. I know little about the Irish and their fight for independence. Being a typical American, most of foreign history and affairs in general are sadly outside of my interest or concern.

Shamus found the only other Irish native at the prison and befriended him. Johnny was his name. Shamus always dominated the conversation, and I don't recall Johnny ever really talking that much.

I would get stuck in their company at the chow hall or waiting for medical appointments, and they even found their way up to the wellness office. Not to join classes or do anything fitness related—just to talk. And the conversation was always about Ireland. "Half these cunts wouldn't last a day in Belfast, they really wouldn't. When you've spent the last fifteen years in the trenches with your fellow IRA brothers, fighting the bloody English back the stinking holes from which they were birthed, then you'll know true hell. This so-called prison ain't nothing more troublesome than grabbing a pint at a pub in Tralee. Ain't that right, Johnny?" Shamus blabbed one day as he smacked Johnny on the arm. Johnny just nodded slowly, not attempting to talk, for he knew he would be cut off mid-sentence if he tried.

Shamus was a pudgy, short fellow with shoulder length brownish blonde hair, a bit on the thinning side. His blotchy complexion and jaundiced eyes led one to believe he'd led less than a healthy lifestyle for some time before winding up there in our corner of the universe. I had a hard time believing he was quite the badass he portrayed himself to be, but I had no interest in testing that theory out.

Johnny was your stereotypical Irish lad. Wiry frame, thin lipped with a narrow nose and flaming red hair. As I've said, he was quiet, but I got the feeling that he could hold his own in a fight if it came to that. Mostly because I have this notion that Irish and English lads are constantly getting into brawls over darts at the pub or feuding with rival fanatics over their favorite football club.

Either way, these two were inseparable, Somehow, Shamus was even able to get Johnny moved to his cell block, a feat which rarely happened, as the counselors who had the authority to make these moves usually had little interest in accommodating prisoner's interests or desires.

Shamus and Johnny were hanging out with us one night in our office in the wellness department while we were discussing the football games that were to be played that weekend. American football, that is. Kim, Eric, myself, and a bookie name Mustafa who had just come by to pick up the slips I had produced for him, were all in discussion when the pair arrived.

"Brady is freaking awesome, I'm not denying that, but he's got his hands full going against Peyton this week," Mustafa proclaimed. "Indianapolis cannot stop the mighty Patriots this year. They're going to break it off in them, deep!" Eric bragged as if he has inside information. "Aye, the Pats are going to win lads, but they'll not cover the spread. That I can guarantee you," Shamus chimed in with his heavy accent. "We're talking football, not soccer mate," Mustafa teased in an attempted Irish accent. "I don't know, he's been right a lot, lately," Johnny said, surprising us all that he actually spoke. "Well, laddy, put your money where your mouth is. You wanna place a bet, you're looking at the man to make it with, right here," Eric pointed to Mustafa as he spoke.

"Alas gents, I find me-self indigent thanks to the feds freezing all me funds for me high crimes and misdemeanors," Shamus explained.

Johnny extracted a book of stamps from his jacket pocket and held it out to Shamus, who glanced between the stamps and Johnny's face for only a moment before he snatched it away. "Alright then, put me down for five dollars on the Colts to cover the spread," Shamus threw the stamps on the desk in front of Mustafa. "Okay, but the payout on a single bet is five to six. You're gonna need another dollar if you want to make a single wager," Mustafa patiently explained.

Shamus backhanded Johnny on the arm. "You heard the man, Johnny. What you waiting for then? Be a lad and go get this huckster a bag of mackerel so we can beat the Americans at their own game, eh?" Johnny looked a little confused as to whether he should be going at that moment or not. Shamus smacked him again in the arm, "That's right. Off with you then, quick like a bunny. There you go," he prodded him like he would a child. Johnny turned and slowly walked out the door, the disbelief that his kind gesture had not only cost him an extra dollar, but also earned him the chore of hiking all the way to his cell to fetch the mackerel was plain on his face.

Johnny returned a short time later, and the deal was sealed. Mustafa wasn't usually one for taking such small bets, nor waiting like he did that night for Johnny to return with a dollar, but I got the impression he just wanted the braggadocious Irishman to be proven wrong and put in his place.

Lo and behold, the Pats won, but did not cover. Shamus wasted no time in tracking down Mustafa the next day once again, in our office in the wellness department. It was, after all, the favorite hangout for a lot of guys.

"Looks like the mick has bested the yanks on this one, eh laddy?" Shamus was smug as he collapsed into the chair in front of Kim's desk. Johnny leaned against the wall beside him.

"Good pick, no question. But even a blind squirrel finds a nut once in a while," Mustafa responded calmly as he fished Shamus's winnings out of the sack he had carried in with him.

Shamus accepted the two books of stamps and one bag of mackerel that Mustafa held out to him, pocketed the two books of stamps, and tossed the mackerel to Johnny without giving him a glance. Johnny fumbled the toss, before eventually securing the catch. He looked at the mackerel, then to the back of Shamus's head incredulously before slipping the bag into his coat pocket. Surely, I wasn't the only one keeping a mental accounting, and wondering how Johnny was getting screwed on this endeavor.

"I'm a student of the game, lad. Luck's got nothing to do with it," Shamus, ever the self-promoter proclaimed.

"Well, Dallas plays tonight. Prove it," Mustafa laid down the gauntlet.

"What's the spread?"

"Oh, I thought you were a student of the game?"

"Well. MacNabb and Westbrook are too much for the Dallas *Cowgirls* to stop, there's not a question about that. By how much? I'd have to see the line to make an educated wager," Shamus pontificated.

"Dallas is giving seven. The over/under is 56," answered Mustafa.

"Dallas is giving seven. Well, I don't go in for that over under/shit, but that's an easy call for sure, laddy." Shamus smacked Johnny on the arm and ordered, "Go get the man another bag of mackerel, Johnny, we're about to show these boys the luck of the Irish." Johnny shook his head in disbelief, but obediently left the office to retrieve the goods to complete the transaction. Upon his return, Shamus handed over two books of stamps, along with two bags of mackerel to Mustafa for the bet. By my account, Johnny was now down seven bucks.

Shamus won, and continued to win each week, doubling his money each week. Well, almost. Every time Shamus placed a bet, Johnny would need to add one bag of mackerel to the pot, which, anticipating this, had begun to bring mackerel with him each time.

By week seven Shamus's winnings equaled one hundred and twenty-eight books of stamps, or $640. Johnny was out seven mackerel and one book of stamps, or $12. All this winning was beginning to cost poor Johnny, that's for sure. Johnny never complained, but the look on his face each time Shamus double downed was plain enough that he'd just as soon take the winnings and be done with it.

When the boys came to collect the winnings in the office, Mustafa was waiting. "I think if you replaced the word 'luck' with 'intelligence', the phrase 'luck of the Irish', might be more appropriate, don't you think, lads?" Shamus bragged as he entered the room and plopped down into the chair in front of my desk. Johnny stood beside him. Mustafa was not happy; we could tell that during the ten minutes he'd been waiting for them to arrive. He'd barely said five words to us.

Mustafa stood with his mesh laundry bag and dumped its contents onto my desk in front of Shamus. "Nobody likes a bragger, Mick," Mustafa said as we all watched the bundles of stamps and mackerel bags tumble onto the table. The books of stamps were in stacks of ten, rubber banded together. "No more bets for you Mick. The word is out, no bookie on the compound will take any future wagers from you. My advice to you is to take your winnings and shut your fucking mouth about it, you dig?" Mustafa's hulking frame towered over the seated Shamus, who wisely raised an eyebrow and nodded his head in agreement. Mustafa gave the rest of us in the room a friendly look and a "good evening gentlemen," before giving Shamus a stink eye look which lasted so long, I thought things might escalate. It did not, and Mustafa simply left the room.

Shamus's eyes remained downcast until Mustafa's footfalls could no longer be heard retreating down the hallway. "Bit of a sore loser, don't ya think?" Shamus said quietly once he thought it safe to do so.

"Yo, dat man, he not fucking around, ok? If he even hears dat you been talking shit, it's not going to be good for you, understand?" Kim admonished while jabbing a pointed finger at him.

Shamus rose and gathered his loot, stuffing the pockets of his pants and coat with the stamps. "Grab your macks, Johnny." Shamus spoke to Johnny like he was a servant, as always. Johnny stuffed the pouches of fish into his pockets as Shamus peeled two books of stamps out from one of the banded stacks and held them out to Johnny. "Here you go then, lad, you've doubled your money." The look on Johnny's face was dubious as he reached out to accept the meager profit. Shamus turned on his heel and left the room, Johnny seemed paralyzed for a moment, then hung his head and followed.

We all felt bad for Johnny, but in prison you have to be able to fight your own battles. Johnny clearly wasn't ready to do that yet.

Some time had passed, and we'd all continued on with our routines. We saw less and less of the two Irishmen, and they never came back to hang out in the office anymore. You'd see them at chow hall and walking across the compound keeping their own company. As usual, when I saw them, Shamus was doing the talking, and Johnny looked dejected.

Word came to us one day that Shamus had been taken to the hospital for some mystery illness. We all joked that Johnny had finally poisoned him, but had there been access to poison in prison, you can imagine how less populated the place would be.

Kim and I ran into Johnny outside the wellness building one night while we waited for the doors to be unlocked. "Yo, Johnny, what happened to Shamus? How's your boy doing?" Kim asked as he approached.

"Hey guys. I don't know. He was feeling a bit under the weather and went to medical one day. I heard from an orderly that works there that they took him out in an ambulance."

"I'll bet you're glad to have a break from him. He can be a bit much, right?" I asked, trying to get Johnny to reveal his feelings on the guy. He didn't take the bait and just said, "He'll pull through. He's a tough bastard. G'night lads," and walked away.

Several more weeks passed until one day I saw Shamus had returned. Johnny was pushing him down the walkway in a wheelchair. I approached to inquire what had happened but was ignored as Shamus was complaining to Johnny about his skills as a caretaker. "Dammit Johnny, do ya have to hit every fucking bump in the whole damn pathway? Me granny could do a mite better job than this ya fucking wanker!"

Some of us spotted the two over the next couple of days, and everyone who saw them described a similar scene. Johnny was obediently pushing Shamus while being berated by him the entire time.

One day we had a storm come in that started as snow in the morning but turned to freezing rain by the time lunch was called over the loudspeaker. It made for miserable conditions with freezing air, wind, and slushy wet snow to tread through. I was sitting at the desk by the window in my cell when I first heard that obnoxious voice of Shamus's three floors down on the road that led to the chow hall. I couldn't hear the words, but the tone was familiar as I looked upon the pair. Shamus had a plastic trash bag covering his legs in the chair to protect him from the elements, and Johnny was pushing him down the steep hill to the chow hall. As I watched, Johnny began to pick up speed, little by little. As the speed increased, Shamus's ranting got louder and more urgent. Soon Johnny was at a full run, and with a final push, let go of the chair. "Ya dirty fecking cuuuuunt!" Were the only clear words I heard from Shamus as his chair went speeding down the hill. It stayed straight for a moment, but quickly began to slide sideways before something caught a wheel and Shamus went flying, head over heels! He slid face down on the slush for an impossible distance before coming to a stop and rolling over into his back with some effort. Johnny calmly walked down to his one-time friend, stood over him and appeared to say something to him before continuing on to the chow hall, leaving Shamus to his fate. Oh, to have been there, and hear what Johnny said!

I continued to watch until some inmates who were passing by took pity on Shamus and got him back into his chair. They pushed him out of sight, and I never saw the two of them again.

I heard that someone had ratted Johnny out and he was taken to the SHU to spend the remaining days of his sentence, then deported back to Ireland. Shamus was transported to another prison, a move they did often to inmates that they thought might still have enemies on the compound.

I ruminated in my journal's pages that it's best to never bite the hand that feeds you. Johnny was a loyal friend, to a fault. Shamus was never anything but cruel and dismissive to him, treating him like his personal servant. An unpaid servant at that! All it would've taken was a kind word now and then, and maybe an occasional thank you, and Johnny might never have turned on him.

Everyone has their breaking point. Johnny took a lot of flak for a long time. So long in fact, that Shamus thought his patience was endless. I imagine that all the harsh words, the stinginess, and the constant belittling, along with the foul weather that day, finally pushed Johnny over the edge.

Again, the principle of humility came to mind. Nobody likes a bragger. Shamus truly had a knack for picking games. If he had been more gracious, and maybe spread his hustle and placed his bets with different bookies every week, he could have continued making money for the duration of the season. As it turns out, Mustafa had made quite the killing himself. After a few weeks of Shamus's winning, Mustafa began using his picks to make his own bets with other bookies. Much larger bets which covered the losses he paid to Shamus by a long shot. So even though Mustafa was making money using Shamus's picks, he couldn't take his attitude any longer.

Which brought to light yet another lesson. No matter how useful you are to someone, there's only so much shit a person is going to take. No one is indispensable.

Chapter Twenty

NOT EVERY DEBT NEEDS TO BE COLLECTED

IT WAS THE BEGINNING of the football season one year, and Kim decided he was going to be a bookie. He didn't do it every season; it was a difficult undertaking with lots of financial risks and lots of work. I found out one day when I arrived at work and settled in behind my desk. "Yo, shorty, you ready for da football season dis year?" He asked with a peculiar enthusiasm in his voice. I assumed he meant if I had lined up the bookies I would be typing up the betting slips for. "Yeah, I got five customers lined up, and there's sure to be another couple to get into the mix as the season progresses," I answered. "I just got you one more, okay?" He told me. "Yeah, sounds good. Just tell him to come and see me and we'll hammer out the details," I replied. "Dat's da best part, he's already here." He smiled and sat back in his chair, letting me know he was back in business. "We going to make a lot of money dis year, okay Danger?" He said as he rubbed his palms together with dollar signs in his eyes. "Alright Kim, whatever you say," I agreed chuckling at his display of explicit greed.

Kim never seemed to be in need of money. How he sustained himself, I had no idea. He never seemed to take any money from any of the guys he helped either, arranging deals of all sorts for many people over the years I spent with him. Kim rarely had anything but information that people wanted. If you needed or wanted something, Kim knew who to put you in touch with to get it.

"Dis time, Danger, you going to help me, okay?" he asked. "Of course, Kim, anything for you." Finally, I could give him something back, and I was happy to do it. "You going to let me use da other bookies' lines so I can make da spreads on my tickets. Dis alright with you?" The lines were a carefully guarded secret, and the bookies were adamant about my not sharing them with anyone. They were acquired through an elaborate code the bookies would use when calling home to their families or friends. Newspapers arrived in the prison weeks after their date of print, so those were of no use. Television might give you the lines on a couple of games, but that only happened on game day, and never on every game. So, it was no small thing Kim was asking of me. "No problem, Kim." What else could I say?

Kim must have had a guilty conscience, because on the first day of business, one of my bookies, Juan, entered the office and handed Kim the lines instead of me. "Here you go, mi amigo. You give to El Peligro here when you done." Clearly, he had struck a deal with Juan. I always chuckled inside at how my nickname had morphed, doesn't "El Peligro" translate into *the* danger?

Anyways, Kim read over the lines and copied them onto a piece of paper, making a few adjustments by a point or two on a few of the games. When he'd finished, he handed them over and I got to work. I had gotten fairly proficient at this, and had both sheets, each with twenty-four tickets printed on them completed in no time at all. When I finished, Kim and I walked down to the CO's office to make copies. Kim would distract the CO into conversation while I made the copies under the guise of some legitimate office work, like flyers or signup sheets. Ten copies of each were made and I left the room, leaving Kim to finish with the subterfuge conversation.

There was a copy machine in the library, but I had to pay for those copies using money loaded onto my ID card that was used like a debit card. Plus, in the library there were plenty of prying eyes, something I liked to avoid.

I was in no serious danger, even if I had been caught. As long as you didn't have stacks of stamps or macks on you, or in your locker, screws would accept a lame excuse like "we just play for pushups."

Kim had me taking bets from those who resided in my cell block. I would never collect money lest I get nabbed and lose not only my good time, but also lose out on all my revenue streams I had going at the time. Eric would do the collecting. I would simply collect the bet slips and hand them over to Kim.

One of the guys who would regularly place bets with me was a guy named Big Pun. He was a choice client because he won often enough to keep him coming back but lost more than he won. Kim had a rule that I wasn't to take any bets that had a payout of more than five hundred dollars, and Big Pun always bet the max, and wanted to bet more.

"Yo Danger, why can't I bet as much as I want? I'm gonna find some other bookie if you can't accommodate me," he told me one day.

"You can if you want, but with us you know you always get paid," I tried to reason with him.

"Just talk to your boy, all right?" Pun pleaded with me.

I talked to Kim about it, and he quickly devised a plan. "Ok Danger, here's what we going to do. Dis guy brings in a lot of money, okay? So, you going to let him bet as much as he wants, but you take anything over the max payout and bet the same bet with another bookie. Dat way if we lose, we don't lose the whole thing."

It was a good plan, and I put it into effect the following week. Big Pun put in a heavy bet, with a payout of over seven hundred dollars. He lost, and even after we paid our debt to the other bookie, Kim still brought in a tidy profit.

The season progressed, and Big Pun won some, but lost more as was his nature. He continued to make bigger and bigger bets each week, but no matter what, I always laid any bets that exceeded our max payout onto other bookies. The system continued to work, and we actually put one bookie out of business in the process on a week when Pun had a big win. The bookie we placed our cover bet with couldn't pay the entire amount, but after a conversation with Kim, some deal was agreed upon, and the routine continued as usual.

One fateful day, Big Pun placed his biggest bet yet, with a payout of over two thousand dollars. I was reluctant to accept the bet, but I trusted in the system, so I agreed and took his betting slip. I immediately set off to find a bookie to lay off the majority of the bet but was thwarted in my plan by the loudspeaker. "All inmates return to your bunks for a standing head count immediately. The compound is hereby closed and on lockdown." *Shit!* I was familiar with this scenario; there would be no laying off of any bets for me, we were stuck with a giant bet that could sink the operation. There was nothing to do but hope for the best.

I returned to my cell and prepared for the oncoming searches of not only our possessions, but of our bodies as well. Our *entire* bodies.

First came the standard head count. The guards would come through two at a time to count us and make sure every inmate was accounted for. There were at least six rounds of this, since the art of counting still eluded the guards. Then came the strip search. Again, two guards came to each cell, had us strip, and perform the well-rehearsed and choreographed maneuvers. "Lift your cock. Lift your balls. Show me behind each ear. Turn around. Show me the bottoms of your feet. Bend over, spread your cheeks and cough," We were ordered by the screws.

Once that humiliation was complete, we were allowed to put on our boxers and head down to the TV rooms to await the completion of the searching of our cells. Cold floors, bare feet, mid-November. You can guess how comfortable that wait was. The TV's were turned off, so there was no way to be sure how long it took before we were allowed to return to our cells, but a conservative estimate would put it at about three hours.

Back in our cells, we began the untangling of our possessions, which were tossed into a giant cone-shaped mass in the center of our cells as usual. Thankfully, I was in a two-man cell which made this task much simpler than it had been when I resided in a twelve-man dorm. Clothing, books, letters, and paperwork, along with packages of various food items, were disentangled by my celly Blake and myself. As I folded my clothes and tucked them back into my locker, I took a moment to use my plastic mirror that was held by a magnet to the side of my locker and hold it up at an angle that would allow me to see into the metal cavity of the locker which housed the latch mechanism. Sure enough, all my books of stamps that I had stashed in there were secure. You could always count the guards being lazy. It was one of the only stash spots available to us, and yet it remained one of the best because it took some effort to be found.

We remained locked down for about a week, not leaving our cells except to use the bathroom and once a week to shower. Evidently someone had been stabbed, and the culprit had yet to be discovered. Word had gotten to me, however, that Pun's bet had in fact lost, which was of great relief to me.

Once the compound was opened, and life had returned to normal, word from Eric came that Big Pun couldn't pay up. "He says that all his money was confiscated in the raid," he told us one night in the office.

Inmates were allowed ten books of stamps and thirty macks maximum in their possession. Those of us who had an amount in excess of this amount would use lots of tactics to offset this overage. One way was to try and stash extra books in their locker like I had done myself. Another way was to rent space in other people's lockers. Indigent inmates were happy to store stamps for a onetime fee, usually just a couple of macks. Another method was to hide your booty wherever you worked, or more daring yet, buried somewhere on the compound. The point is, people who had money never kept it all in one place, making Pun's claim doubtful, if not a complete fairy tale.

To my astonishment, Kim took the news well, sitting back in his chair in the office with hands clasped together, fingers steepled against his lips in contemplation. "Okay. Just put out the word dat he owes, and nobody take his bet until he pays, alright?" Kim handed down the verdict, which I thought rather light. "Kim, you going to let him get away with this? You know he's full of shit!" I argued. "Oh, don't worry Danger, he pay. He think he got away with something, but he going to pay a lot more than he ever thought" I was flabbergasted! In all my years of doing time, I'd never seen a debt go unpaid or unpunished! This type of non-response would undoubtedly set Kim up as an easy mark, or so I thought.

Pun stayed to himself for a few days, not even going to the chow hall. Most likely sustaining himself on ramen noodles and whatever else he had in his locker. He eventually emerged and I saw him in line at dinner one night. Trays were assembled behind a stainless-steel barrier as we moved through the line where they would be handed to us at the end. It was chicken night; we always got a leg quarter, which sounds good, right? Well, the size of these chickens led one to believe they had been harvested prematurely to say the least. I glanced over to Pun's tray as he collected it and saw that there was a big bite out of his already anemic looking bird. His sides of peas and carrots equaled about a tablespoon size scoop, and his slice of bread had a big thumb dent in the middle. Pun looked at his food, and for a moment I'm sure he thought about complaining to the kitchen staff guard, but that would be ratting, so he took his pathetic meal and shuffled off.

As I went looking for a seat, I saw Pun being turned away from table after table, nobody wanted him at theirs. He eventually leaned against the wall next to the tray return window and ate while balancing his tray with one hand. It didn't take long, since he was barely given any food to begin with.

This went on for about a week. No one would allow Pun in their presence. Whether it was the TV room, card tables, or just being in their general proximity anywhere on the compound. Pun couldn't go to the commissary because that would require money, and if he had money, he would have to pay his debts first.

Word finally came that he turned himself into the SHU. Who knows what story he gave them, but if you told them, you were in danger, they would take you off the compound and throw you in the SHU. Eventually, if you were lucky, they would transfer you somewhere else. At Fort Dix they had two compounds, an Eastside, and a Westside. The two were completely separate from one another, and history had shown that a guy in this situation was usually transferred to the opposite one after about six months in the hole. However, even if he did make it there, news always seemed to follow him in time. Sucked to be him!

I wrote in my journal on how it appeared that not every debt needs to be collected. Sure, nobody likes to be cheated out of money, but Big Pun was paying a heavy price in the end. Nobody would have anything to do with him afterwards. He was a known cheat, an outcast. He was relegated to the status of the other losers and low-lifes that were not fit to mingle with the general population: pedophiles, rats, and rapists. A real scarlet letter situation if you will.

Sometimes it would cost you more to collect in the end. If Kim had stripped him of all he had—radios, headphones, etcetera—the debt would be considered paid and life for Big Pun would've carried on as before. If he had him beaten up, or worse, there was a distinct chance Big Pun would rat and that would've caused a whole lot of headaches. The CO's would only be tolerant of Kim's doings if there wasn't any trouble. Besides, if inmates' activities did not lead to violence or other disruptive behavior, a blind eye was generally turned to activities that kept us occupied and out of the hair of the prison staff.

Chapter Twenty-One

IT NEVER HURTS TO ASK

Even thugs can be reasonable. I had recently been moved to a new building so that I could begin a substance abuse program I had enrolled in. You had to live in this building to take the course since all the classes were held there, and that way they wouldn't be compromised during lockdowns or movement between buildings being suspended.

I was assigned a top bunk in a twelve-man cell, along with a diverse group of guys. Directly across from me on a bottom bunk was a fella named Jamal who always cracked me up with his butchery of the English language. He fancied himself an aficionado of jewelry but couldn't pronounce it to save his life. "Jewry" was the way it came out when he spoke, and he spoke it often, always steering conversations back to his favorite topic. I thought to myself, "Maybe Jewry was accessories for Jewish people?" Other phrases he was especially fond of mangling were" Better safe *and* sorry," and "You playing rush *and* roulette."

Another inhabitant was Jerry. He slept on the top bunk to my left. A gentleman in his late fifties who had some form of Tourette's I assume, for whenever he spoke, his sentences were interspersed with funny sounds accompanied by facial tics. A typical conversation with Jerry would go something like, "Umm, keh-snnf, Danger, look, kuh, what I, snft, found in the trash...kmft, four newspapers, kah, from Delaware!" Jerry also had a collection of seeds he was attempting to germinate in his locker. He had extracted these from tomatoes and peppers and put them between moist tissue paper that was placed in a plastic lid. Thankfully, they never sprouted because he never would have been allowed to plant or harvest them anyways. Doing time effects everyone differently, and this is how Jerry chose to deal with it.

There was a kid named Mark who resided in the bottom bunk just inside the door to our cell. He was a lanky, blonde-haired dude in his early twenties. He was a quiet loner who rarely spoke to anyone but passed his time drawing pictures on his bunk. He was quite the artist too. I would occasionally glance down from my bunk at his work and see fantastical drawings of demons, dragons and all sorts of fantasy-based characters, really amazing stuff.

One day he strolled into the cell in a determined manner and began to set up shop at the table located at the far end of the room. I was laying on my bunk trying to expand my literary horizons by reading some classic, I think it was *The Brothers Karamazov* or *Fear and Loathing*, something challenging enough without a distraction. I found myself really just peering over my book to spy on Mark's goings on. First, he set out a small empty plastic bottle which he then filled with olive oil which could be purchased from the commissary. Next, he poked a hole through the lid using a nail he must have acquired from one of the maintenance guys. Through that hole he threaded a piece of a shoelace. He's making a candle I surmised, for what reason I could not imagine. He then covered the lid with a piece of aluminum foil he undoubtedly procured from the mess hall, with the wick poking through. He lit the candle and got it burning with a plume of black soot billowing into the air. He then held a magazine with a glossy cover above the plume and let the soot collect on the cover. It only took a few moments for the magazine to be completely covered in chalky blackness. He blew out the candle and quickly dismantled his candle set up before any turnkey could walk in on him. Once the candle paraphernalia was put away, he sat down at the desk and scraped the soot off into a plastic bowl using the edge of his ID card. Then he slowly stirred in shampoo while mixing the compound with the end of a pen. Once he felt he had the right consistency, he poured the liquid into another empty plastic bottle, cleaned up his mess and left the room. I was perplexed but knew that eventually I would come to know what all this was about.

Over the next couple of days, I saw Mark working on some sort of electronics. He would have a bunch of components spread out on a towel, which he would fold one end over his project to conceal it every time the door opened to our cell. Soon the project was completed, and with the attachment of a couple of AA batteries, his tattoo gun sprang to life. Aha! I thought, I should have known. He quickly concealed the tattoo gun and ink that he'd made from the soot and shampoo into the leg of the table we all shared in the room.

In no time at all Mark had a booming business "slinging ink," as he liked to call it. There were clients coming at almost every gate unlock to get work done. At the end of the day's sessions, Mark would unscrew the table leg and place his contraband inside before reattaching the leg. It was a decent strategy all things considered.

First, there weren't many hiding spots in the prison that the guards had not already figured out. Secondly, if it weren't in any one person's locker, it couldn't be pinned on anyone. Or so he thought!

About a month into Mark's little enterprise, we had some random cell tosses in the building and ours was one of the cells selected. And wouldn't you know it, they found Mark's stash. After we'd been allowed back into our cell to sort through the pile of our commingled belongings in the center of the room, it was quickly discovered that the jig was up. In short order we heard all of our names over the intercom being summoned to the lieutenant's office on the other side of the compound.   We all looked at each other with a shoulder shrug and headed off to meet our fate.

"They can't pin dat shit on none of us, man," Jamal began reasoning as we walked. "Yeah, it's a common area. Anyone could have put that there. Hell, it could have been there for years for all they know," Mark added. This banter continued the entire five-minute walk to the lieutenant's office as the fellas tried to reassure themselves that everything was going to be ok. I kept silent, knowing that on the streets and in a court of law we might have stood a chance, but this was prison.

We shuffled into the waiting room of the lieutenant's office and plopped ourselves into the hard plastic chairs that lined the walls. All conversation had ceased once we'd reached the building. A sergeant came out to call us in three at a time. "Inmates Gilford, Johnson, and Duarte, follow me," he beckoned. We three followed him through a door where he then directed us separately into three different rooms. I found myself sitting in a chair across from a lieutenant with slicked back jet-black hair and a giant guardsman mustache who sat behind his desk with my file folder set before him. "Mr. Gilford, welcome. My name is Lieutenant Dance. Let's see what we have here," he began as he flipped open the file. I knew it was a production, but I let it play out as he perused my file. Once he'd finished glancing through all the papers, he closed the file, sat back in his chair, and leveled his gaze at me. "Five-year ten-month sentence for cooking meth," the lieutenant began. "You'll get eight months cut off your sentence if you complete the drug program. Now if we throw you in the hole, you lose your good time. So, what's it going to be? You want to tell me whose tattoo gun and ink was hidden in the leg of the table?" I'm usually a stickler for getting the facts right, but in this situation, I decided to let it go that I only had seven months on my sentence left, with another month of classes still to go. So, at most, I'd only be getting six months off, but there was no sense in arguing semantics.

"Sorry, it's not mine and I don't know who it belongs to."

"You mean to tell me you never saw anyone either giving tattoos or unscrewing a giant table leg in your room, right next to your bunk to stash shit away?" He asked with a sudden arching of a single eyebrow.

I held his gaze and replied, "nope."

He looked down at his desk and moved my file to the bottom of a stack of files before telling me, "I guess we're done here. Tell the sergeant to send in the next one."

In short order we all had our turns giving the same answers to the same questions: we didn't do it, and we didn't know who did. Once we were all gathered back in the waiting room the lieutenant came out to address as a group. "Okay gentlemen, here's the deal. I want you all to go outside for a few minutes to discuss the situation amongst yourselves, away from prying ears. Either the person responsible comes forward to take their lumps, or you all will spend the next 30 days in the hole. You'll lose your good time and the drug program in the process. I'll give you, oh let's say, ten minutes." He motioned towards the door, and we all walked out into the cool dark night.

"Well guys, what do you think?" Mark asked as soon as we were all gathered. I had a little surge of hope in my chest. "I don't do the cop's job for them, we go hard," Jamal chimed in, extinguishing that spark of hope that had just lit for me. The others all had their say, echoing Jamal's statement almost verbatim. I could see in their eyes that their words were in complete conflict with their hearts. "What about you, Danger, what do you think?" Mark asked me. I took a deep breath, crafting my words carefully in my head before speaking. If I wasn't careful, I could be seen as breaking the prison code of solidarity. "Well, here's how I see it," I began, making sure to look each man in the eyes as I spoke. "If it were me, I wouldn't take my cellmates down with me for something they had nothing to do with." I saw some heads begin the shake side to side and quickly added, "However, I would never rat out another man for any reason, and if you decide to ride it out and see if we can't win on appeal, I'll ride with you 'til the wheels fall off." Nobody had a chance for rebuttal, and Mark certainly didn't have time to ponder my words because the lieutenant came out from the office at exactly that moment. "Okay gentlemen, time's up. What have we decided?" Dance barked as the other screws followed him out and began circling our group. My stomach sank. Now I wasn't so concerned about the good time, but of all the "compound cash" I had stashed in my and other people's lockers throughout the prison. I had roughly $500 worth of stamps and bags of mackerel that was intended to be traded for actual cash to be sent to my books for when I was released to help me until I could find work. The going exchange rate was 75 cents on the dollar.

To my utter shock, Mark spoke up. "You don't need to involve these guys; it was my tattoo gun and ink."

"Good man. You other fellas can head back to your housing unit." Lieutenant Dance instructed us. A sigh of relief swept over me, though I still felt apprehension over what the guys thought of my little speech. Jamal leaned in as we walked. "Way to go, Danger, you saved our asses on that one." The others all voiced their gratitude as well, I even received a few pats on the back. One guy told me, "Man, you said what we were all thinking." I thought, "Well I'm like the least badass dude in the group, why didn't one of them have the guts to say something?"

I don't have any journal entries for that evening, so it must have been a revelation that sunk in over time. I did, however, come to realize that having the courage of your convictions can be extremely hard, but extremely rewarding. So many things in prison can be taken the wrong way and have serious consequences. Inmates tend to read a lot into your words, always looking for the hidden meaning or ulterior motives. Words must be chosen with care.

None of those guys wanted to "go hard" and take the fall for Mark's shit, but were all afraid like I was that they would be seen as soft at best, or on the verge of ratting at worst. Sometimes your words may be the one that gives voice to what everyone else is already thinking.

Chapter Twenty-Two

PEOPLE LOVE A COMEBACK STORY

As I was counting down the days to my release from prison, I had countless worries and things to consider. Thankfully, money—at least in the short term—was not one of those worries. Due to all of my entrepreneurial activities, mostly owed to Kim's guidance, I had several thousand dollars saved up to cover my expenses until I could get on my feet. Getting on my feet was of great concern. For the first six months I knew I would be going to a halfway house, so that eased my mind somewhat. However, once I left the halfway house, I would be under the gun. My mother's lease would only allow for guests to stay with her for two weeks at a time—not long for a parolee to get on his feet!

Mom had devised a plan where I could stay with her for two weeks at a time, then go to a motel for two weeks, and just keep repeating the cycle until I found housing. This was the most criminal idea my mother had ever thought of; I was so proud of her. However, I was determined to have my own place at the end of that first two weeks. The execution of that desire was somewhat in question.

After all, I had never rented anything on my own in my life. Oh, and my credit score was lingering in the low 500's with nothing but unpaid debts and broken promises to show for my 38 years on this planet. Would I be able to find work being an ex-con with a giant gap in my employment history? I was armed with two letters of recommendation from previous employers. Sure, they were a bit dated, but at least there had been a period in my life where two people had thought enough of me to put down in writing that they thought I was worthy of employment. I honestly believed through faith in God that things would work out, but I also knew that I had to do the leg work and be steadfast in my tenacity at pursuing these things.

On the morning of my release, I rose from a fitful sleep to the PA speaker, "Standing head count! All inmates stand beside your bunks and prepare for head count!" *Last time I'll have to hear that!* I thought. Once the count was cleared, I stripped my bed for the final time, took the bedding, towels, and my uniforms down to the laundry and dropped it all off before heading to the chow hall where I met up with Kim and Eric.

There we dined on a fine cuisine of runny scrambled eggs, burnt stale toast and a very unripe slice of cantaloupe. I was glad for the awful food, as it was yet another reminder of how sweet freedom would be. We chatted not only about my plans, but those we shared on some business ideas on how to capitalize on our shared prison experiences. Kim's ideas, I should clarify, which Eric and I would try and facilitate from the outside.

Once we'd finished our meals, we headed back to my cell block where I retrieved all my worldly possessions, which consisted of paperwork and some toiletries. To the fellas I turned over all my compound cash—120 books of stamps and 30 bags of mackerel—and a few radios with headphones. There were some other items like a fairly new pair of Timberland boots which could fetch a handsome price on the compound and various gym related items like workout gloves and lifting straps. The boys were happy to receive them, and then Kim surprised me with a parting gift of his own.

"Yo Danger, let's walk up to the account monitor and check your balance," he suggested. "I checked it last night. I have $3,082.18," I replied.

"Yo shorty, why you always have to argue with me huh? Let's just go and see," he retorted. I acquiesced and we made the trek from outside my cell block and up to the commissary building where, mounted to a wall under a portico, was a video monitor where inmates could check their account balances. To my surprise, my balance now read over $5,000! "What's this?" I asked.

"Yo shorty, I just wanted to make sure you gonna make it out there. Money goes a lot faster than you think, okay?" What could I do but say "thank you", followed by the socially acceptable bro hug where we clasped hands while leaning in to touch shoulders briefly, thereby showing gratitude and friendship in a completely heterosexual manner.

We said our final goodbyes outside the R&D building once the CO poked his head out from the door and called my name along with a half dozen other lucky souls. I was cautiously excited and nervous. I had been in this position once before, only to find out moments before my release that there was still an outstanding warrant for my arrest on new charges, so I was prepared for the worst, as is my tendency.

I shuffled in with the group of guys where the officers locked us up into two separate holding cells and sorted out our paperwork. Everyone was jubilant about what they were going to do first, and optimistic about their chances of making it on the outside. I knew from not only my own history, but by the number of guys I'd seen leave, only to return a short time later, that at least half of this group would be back before the Earth could complete its journey around the sun. I prayed I would not be one of them.

One by one we were called out to a desk where we were told of our travel plans, where we would be going, by which mode of transportation we would be traveling, which rules we had to follow, and what time we had to report to our halfway house or to our PO's for those not going to a halfway house. We signed countless documents, and we were handed $200 each for travel and food. Also, we received a check with the remaining balance on our accounts. I was feeling more optimistic by now. I mean, they wouldn't hand me money if I wasn't going to be released! Once we were back in the holding cells, we had a long wait before anything else transpired. My confidence waned as the minutes ticked by. My brain always goes to the worst possible outcome. I should have been prepared for the wait. If prison teaches you anything, patience is it. Nothing happens quickly or efficiently in prison. Life on the inside is a constant waiting game. Waiting for the compound to open, waiting for the call for chow hall, waiting for your parole date, standing in line for hours for everything from medical needs to commissary.

Finally, we were all called out into a big open area where we were given our dress out packages that our families had mailed to us. We eagerly opened our boxes and began changing into our street clothes, depositing our prison-issued khakis and underclothes into a laundry basket. I'm at a loss for words to describe how it felt to slip on soft boxers and socks. Prison clothing was so scratchy it was like it was made from sandpaper. I slid on my new jeans and a crisp button up shirt. It was amazing! I looked around the room to inspect my comrades' choices of fashion and instantly made judgements as to their likelihood of violating probation. I know they say don't judge a book by its cover, but some of these book covers had hoodlum written all over them!

At this point they marched us across the compound, through the visitation center and to another holding cell just one door away from freedom. As we walked along our path, we got catcalls and shouts of well wishes from inmates we passed and from those at the windows of their cell blocks. I'd seen this scenario from their perspective so many times before that it was surreal to be the one making the journey myself this time, as if my feet were floating two inches off the ground. Once we had all been corralled into the holding cell, we were subjected to another exasperatingly long wait while the screws double checked their paperwork to make sure they were letting out the right people at the right time. The process was no doubt made much more stringent due to an inmate from another prison being released a few months earlier who was supposed to be serving a life sentence! Oops.

One by one they called us up to what resembled the ticket booth at a movie theater, complete with the circular hole in the middle to speak through, and a rectangular slot at the bottom to pass paperwork back and forth through. They quizzed us on our names, dates of birth, prison registration numbers, and a number of other things, until they were sure we were who we said we were. Eventually we all passed our final tests and were let outside the prison gates for the first time in who knows how long for my companions, but five years for me! The air smelled cleaner, the sun shone brighter, and it felt like a breath I'd been holding all this time was finally exhaled! Ahhh.

We loaded into an extended van and began the ride through the maze of the Fort Dix military base. It turns out the prison was situated smack dab in the center of this army base. Even if some poor soul had figured out a way to escape the prison, he would still have had miles of a military labyrinth to navigate to find his way to freedom! At the edge of the base the van pulled to a stop in a parking lot to let two of our fellow discharges off so they could be taken away by their family members who were there waiting. From there we were driven to several bus stations, letting off one or two probationers at each until myself and one other fellow were the final two. We were deposited at some roadside bus station in Trenton, New Jersey with all the pomp and circumstance of the trash being dumped at the corner. We were on our own with no supervision for the first time. I was nervous, excited, and even a little scared. I was especially worried I would miss my bus, or a connection, or that we'd been dropped off too late to make our bus. Like I said, my mind always takes me to the worst-case scenario, that way anything else is a win! My companion was a fellow named Jose. He was familiar with the area and knew how to navigate the transit system, so I followed his lead. We walked up to the man in the ticket booth, who took a glance at our prison ID's. We bought our tickets and walked outside to wait for our bus. The station attendant appeared to be familiar with seeing prison ID's and made no fuss while we transacted our business. That was one of my worries put to rest.

While we waited outside in the chilly November air, I had a chance to witness some of the fairer sex in their natural habitat. They looked so clean and pretty. I must have been staring a bit too long because I got a nudge from Jose who didn't look at me, he just said, "Take a glance then move on. You're making it obvious." Oops.

Our bus finally arrived, and Jose and I settled in for our trip into New York City and Grand Central Station, (Or was it the Port Authority? Either way, it was big). This was my second trip to New York; my first was as a prisoner shackled in the back of a bus. This time would be as a semi-free man, in a much nicer bus. Country boys like me must stand out like sore thumbs, all wide eyed, taking in all the sights. I was amazed at all the people in such close proximity to one another. I couldn't imagine how people live like that. The noise was another thing. It was like sensory overload, and yet I knew that the quiet of the country would probably be just as unnerving to them as the city was to me.

I was once again thankful for Jose as we disembarked from the bus. This maze of underground terminals and passageways was dizzying to me, but Jose led the way as if he could navigate this madness in his sleep. The mass of humanity that crowded around us was giving me anxiety, but there was nothing to do but move forward. We arrived at our terminal and once again, we waited.

I had time to observe the people in my proximity, and began one of my favorite pastimes, imagining what brought these people here, and what was going on in their lives. There was a White man in a suit, leaning up against a wall with his blazer hung over one arm. A briefcase at his feet while he was engrossed in some paperwork he continuously flipped back and forth through. He was an attorney, I thought. He was looking for inconsistencies to make his case while he waited for the bus to take him to the courts.

Seated on the floor a few feet away from him was a Black man, either homeless or near to it. His hair was a mess, his clothing dirty and in tatters. He looked as though he smelled badly, though he was too far for me to confirm it, thankfully! I felt he was at the tail end of a string of bad turns of events. He was waiting for the bus to take him to his one last chance at turning his whole life around.

Across the way, huddled in a corner with her two small children stood a nervous Latina woman who distractedly kept touching her kids' heads and shoulders as if to reassure herself that they were still there while she prattled on about their plight. "We've spent the last of our money on these tickets, kids, I hope Mom finds work soon," I overheard her saying a bit too loudly. Clearly, she was an out of towner as well, trying to convince any would-be muggers that she would make a poor target.

Our bus to Boston arrived, and we boarded with the rest of the crowd. There was some confusion as to whether or not there was enough room for all the passengers to fit on the bus, which briefly sent the fear of being left behind coursing through my system. A few moments for the counting of bodies, and we were allowed onto the bus. One more bullet dodged.

Jose took a nap on the ride to Boston, but my eyes were glued to the surroundings outside my window as we traveled through New York, Connecticut, and finally into Massachusetts. When we got to Boston I was amazed when we passed over the Leonard P. Zakim Bridge. The Sox had just won the World Series, and the city was electric. I could feel it through the window of the bus. Buildings had their window lights spelling out things like "Go Sox" and "Champs" which blazed brightly against the night sky.

Jose and I got off the bus in Boston and called a cab. We made sure we had enough cash to cover the trip to Lawrence and headed off on our final leg of our journey. Jose and I had a brief disagreement about whether or not to trip the driver, but in the end, I prevailed, and he got a ten-dollar tip from each of us for an hour's drive to Lawrence.

When we got to the halfway house, we found that we were to be residing in a three-story Victorian placed behind an eight-foot chain link fence, topped with razor wire. So much for leaving prison.

We checked in with the guards and made our way into our new home. Once inside and settled in, I was happy to see a few of my comrades who had been at Fort Dix before me. The Brain being one of them. I nicknamed him "The Brain" back when we used to play rummy in the cell block. I wasn't particularly good at first and The Brain would gloat about his superior intellect. "You see, LB, I have a giant brain. You have a little brain. That's why I always win." He called me "LB," short for Little Brain. After some time, I came to know his style of playing, and his tells. So, I began to win. We kept score, and the loser of the week had to buy the ice cream at the commissary. It was a fun and relatively inexpensive way to gamble. Once I had bested him a few weeks in a row, I began my own bit of trash talking. "What's the matter, Brain, is your giant brain not working this week?"

Jimmy, a friend from the cell next to The Brain's would stop by during our ice cream socials and ask, "Who bought the ice cream this week, The Brain?" And so, the nickname was solidified.

So, I was glad to see The Brain, and he was able to give me the lay of the land. "LB, this place is crazy, but because we're feds, we get some liberties. First thing you need to know is, they have a count once every hour from 6am to 9pm. I call it 'hide the count' because you never know where in this place they're going to have it. I just wait a few minutes until all these county inmates have figured out where it is, then once you see them coming back to their rooms you can just ask them where it's at. Second thing is you have to go see Sergeant Jenkins first thing in the morning and tell him you're a new fed and you need a job; he'll hook you up. Finally, after you've seen Jenkins, go to the third floor and find Lieutenant Abraham. Tell him you just got in and you need to go shopping for clothes and whatnot. Make sure you buy good winter clothes because you don't know if the job you get will be outside or not. Oh, and one other thing, when they drop you off to do your shopping, there's a TGI Fridays at the strip mall, grab yourself a steak or something, but be careful! I sliced open my thumb with a steak knife! Turns out six years of only using a plastic spork for meals have dulled my skills for using cutlery!"

The next day, after my first "hide the count" (it was in the basement this time) I checked in with both Jenkins and Abraham. Before long I was being chauffeured in a county van to the local strip mall. "Pick you up right here in two hours. Don't be late," the officer told me as he sped away from the curb. This was the first time I had been truly alone and untethered for five years. I just stood there on the sidewalk and let the sunlight warm my face in the chilly New England air for a few minutes. I checked my watch: 11:30am. I decided to just walk the length of the mall to see which stores I had to choose from. TJ Maxx, Walmart, Barnes and Noble, and Home Depot. Across the parking lot sat the TGI Fridays. *I'll do you last,* I thought.

This is it, I thought to myself as I walked into the TJ Maxx. *I'm starting from scratch. I can build this life however I choose, starting with my wardrobe.* It was an amazing feeling to be alone, browsing through items and picking out my own clothes for the first time in five years.

By the time I was done shopping I had two giant bundles of bags with all sorts of clothing, toiletries, and a few books that I had been wanting to read, but were unavailable in the prison library. I lugged my purchases over to the restaurant and sat in a booth, my bags filling the bench across the table from me.

I took my time perusing the menu. After all, I still had an hour before my ride. Before I got there, I had planned to order the steak, but in the end, I chose a cheeseburger with Jack Daniels Barbecue sauce. It was delicious! Afterward, I worried that there may have been a detectable amount of alcohol in that sauce, but I reassured myself that if I didn't feel any effects, then it was probably fine.

Upon my return to "The Farm," as my residence was referred to, I learned from Jenkins that I had been given a job, and I was to start that night. It was a third shift job at a fine dessert factory that supplied desserts to high end restaurants throughout New England.

For about a month I worked at this sweatshop with a handful of guys from The Farm. They would bus us up every night at ten o' clock, and there we would toil until dawn. Sometimes I would be loading heavy drums of frosting into a hopper that the cake decorators would extract from a hose on the assembly line at an amazing pace. The cakes would move down a conveyor belt, then spin on a turntable while folks applied frosting and spread it smooth with a knife.

Another time I was taking cakes off a conveyor belt that was coming out of a giant oven. I would flip the cakes out of their pans onto another conveyor belt and stack the pans on a cart. The supervisor had forgot about me, and I was stuck behind that hot oven flipping cakes and stacking pans all night without a break! There was no way to shut off the power, and the cakes came out of the oven so fast that I didn't even have time to go to the bathroom. It was like that classic scene from I Love Lucy when she's in the chocolate factory. I couldn't believe that no one ever came to that side of the oven so I could ask for help.

I had long ago run out of carts to stack them on, so I just started piling them on the floor. The supervisor finally found me twenty minutes after quitting time because the guards from The Farm were looking for me, and he was shocked to see me surrounded by hundreds of cake pans stacked in six-foot piles all around me. It looked as though I were building a fort with them! The supervisor was very apologetic, and the next night let me take an hour and a half break. He even bought me dinner.

The job wasn't all bad. Most of the people who worked there were Hispanic, and most of those were women. They were extremely sweet, and when they saw the pathetic bagged lunches we were provided with, they took pity on us—or maybe they saw a way to make a few extra bucks—and offered to make us dinners each night for $20 a week. Five bucks a day for authentic Puerto Rican and Dominican cuisine? Oh, hell yeah!

One guy declined their offer saying, "I don't trust these spics!"

"You don't trust these sweet ladies over the disgusting mystery meat they put in our sandwiches from The Farm? You got issues, dude," I told him plainly.

The gig didn't last long, however. A couple of the county fellas from The Farm were caught drinking beers they had gotten someone to supply them with at the factory, and our jobs were terminated on the spot. It's just as well, because working all night did not excuse me from having to make the count every hour on the hour back at the Farm. So, I never really got any sleep.

My next job that I was given was working in a massive old factory building that was being converted into luxury condos. There would usually be between four and eight of us on the crew. We weren't the ones doing the construction; we were only there to clear out debris and junk left behind from when the factory was in operation.

The best part of this job was that there was a gym my buddy and I could use on our lunch breaks, so I wouldn't lose all those gains I'd worked so hard for during my bid.

One of our coworkers was nicknamed Andre the Machete. He was a hilarious Dominican man with a heavy accent, a bald head, and a short, stocky frame. One of his favorite phrases which he often used was "See you later, alligator." He had never heard the proper response to that, until we were working around the opening of an abandoned elevator shaft on the fourth floor one day.

He looked over the edge of the shaft and saw how far down the fall would be. "Oh no, no, no. Danger I cannot do dis, señor! I see you later alligator!"

"Ok, after a while crocodile," I responded.

"What? What is dis, 'after a while crocodile'?" His mind was blown, and he was so happy to have this new addition to his favorite phrase.

Another time he was in the gym with us lifting some weights. He was strong as a bull, and after bench pressing some ridiculous amount of weight, he sprung to his feet and proclaimed, "I need some water. My body has a way of letting me know when it needs water!" We all cracked up and I told him "Andre, that's called being thirsty! All of our bodies tell us when we need water, it's not a superpower!"

I continued to work there for the remainder of my halfway house time. The supervisor even gave me a letter of recommendation on my last day and I was happy to have a more recent one under my belt as I headed out into the real world. Surprisingly that night I slept like a baby. I was packed and waiting by the front door when my mom arrived to pick me up the next morning. We drove straight to Concord, New Hampshire so I could check in with my PO. Along the way I snacked on lemon pecan bars, my favorite dessert which Mom had baked for me to celebrate. They were as delicious as I remembered them to be. I washed them down with plenty of water, knowing they would want me to pee in a cup for them when I arrived. I always had to overdo it on the water. If I weren't ready to absolutely burst, I couldn't pee when someone was watching.

When I got to the office, I was surprised to see that my PO was a Barbie-doll-looking officer. Not your stereotypical PO by any means.

I knew she would be extra tough, just to prove that she meant business. Her first show of dominance was to make me wait to take my urine analysis. "Any chance you could take my urine sample first? I chugged a lot of water on my way here to be sure I could go for you guys," I asked as soon as we met.

"You'll have to wait until a male officer is available," she replied flatly. "Follow me."

I did as instructed, and as we snaked our way between desks and cubicles, I couldn't help but notice all the guys standing around chatting with their fellow officers. She didn't even attempt to ask one of them to collect my sample. *Called it!*

We sat down in her office and went through the litany of rules I had to follow, papers I had to sign, and finally my plans on making it on the outside.

"Okay, Mr. Gilford, tell me what your plan is to get a job, find housing, and most of all, stay clean?"

"Well, Ms. Granderson, first of all I plan to spend eight hours a day searching for jobs. I will go to the local employment security office to see what resources they have available. I will use the computer at the library to search for and apply for jobs. I will look in the newspaper for job listings and apply for those jobs that I am qualified for. I figure until I get a job, looking for one is my job, which is why I made myself a vow to spend eight hours a day searching for work. Every time I apply for a job, I will check back with them the next day to show my enthusiasm, and if I don't hear back, I will check in again in a few more days. As for housing, I've never rented a place on my own, and my credit is in the tank, but I will put in the same effort in finding housing as I do to the job search and eventually, I'll land something.

I can only stay at my mom's for two weeks at a time, so I may have to bounce back and forth between her place and a motel until I find something."

"I'm going to stop you right there," she interrupted. "There's no way I'm letting you bounce around between motels and your mother's place. You need to have a permanent residence, where I know I can find you."

"Well, what am I supposed to do if I can't find a place in two weeks?" I asked, genuinely looking for an answer. What I got was, "Figure it out."

As for my staying clean, I told her I would be attending Narcotics Anonymous meetings regularly, to which she reluctantly gave me a pass on the "no associating with known felons" rule, since a lot of the people in those meetings are just that.

Finally, after an hour of her laying down the rules, and raising her eyebrows at each of my plans for success, I was allowed to give a male officer my urine sample. As always, I had trouble going, even though I had to pee so bad I felt like I was doing internal damage. There's just something about peeing in front of someone that locks me up. I'm not ashamed of my body, but when another man's eyes are boring a whole through my junk...

I was able to trickle out enough urine for the sample and was allowed to leave. Immediately after leaving the probation office, I found a restroom in the hall where I could go and empty my bladder in peace. Here, in solitude, my urine stream was so powerful I thought I might chip the porcelain of the urinal!

Mom and I had an hour's drive to get to her home, and on the way, she said to me, "Kevin, I know you're in a hurry to get going on finding a job, but I would really like you to take a week to just decompress and settle into life. The Lord will provide. It's all going to work out." In my head I thought *"Are you crazy? This chick is all over me like white on rice! I have two weeks to find work, and a place to live"* But I simply said, "Okay, Mom, but we have to at least try and find housing, she's not going for the motel idea." Mom agreed to that as long as I promised to relax for one week.

It was hard. I'd been waiting five years for freedom and had planned every hour of my first two weeks out down to the minute, and here Mom was throwing a monkey wrench in my plans. Why this week of not doing anything, I don't know, but I did it the best I could.

In the end, that week did help me to do some things that I wouldn't have been able to do so easily had I been working a full-time job. So, my first order of relaxation was to go to the tanning salon. I felt so pale, like I'd been living in a cave; I needed something to make me feel like I blended in with the other free citizens of Earth. While Mom was at work, I also spent a lot of time walking around the town to get my bearings and see all the new developments that had transpired since I was last there. There had been a lot of changes; we had a Home Depot and a Circuit City now!

I also spent time in the library on the computer setting up an email account, drafting and printing copies of my resume, and basically reveling in this thing called the World Wide Web. It was probably around back when I first got locked up back in 2003, but I had never owned a computer on the streets, and we had no access to it on the inside. Now anything I could think of could be at my fingertips. Thankfully, I had taken several years of computer literacy on the inside, so I was able to complete my tasks without having to ask for help.

Another goal I was able to accomplish was getting my driver's license reinstated. I hadn't had a valid license since 1999! I knew I would do well on the written portion of the test since I had been studying the handbook in the halfway house for six months. It was the driving test that gave me some anxiety. New England roads and drivers are a lot different than California ones. I was unsure about roundabouts for one thing. (Do I use a blinker when exiting a traffic circle?) And what about parallel parking? I hadn't done that since I was sixteen!

I need not have worried; I'll give you the play by play from the test: "Okay, Mr. Gilford, turn left onto the highway. Turn left at this next light. Turn left at this next intersection. Turn left once again. Turn left into the DMV parking lot. Okay, you passed." That was it!

While Mom was at work one day, I was walking around the town, just checking things out, enjoying the fresh air and freedom. I happened to be walking by a laundromat, and for some reason I walked inside. I had no laundry to do, or reason to go in, but I did. It was a small affair, just a single row of washers, flanked by dryers set into the walls. There was a cork bulletin board hanging on the wall with all sorts of flyers dangling from it by thumbtacks. I walked over to it, and quickly focused on the one that read, "Room for rent, shared kitchen and bath, $125 a week."

I dialed the number on my newly acquired cell phone, and heard a phone begin to ring behind the closed office door to my left.

"Old Town Laundromat," came the man's voice over the phone.

"Hi, my name is Kevin. I'm calling about the room for rent."

"Oh, are you here now?"

"Yeah, I'm standing in the laundromat."

The top half of the Dutch door to the office swung open and we both hung up our phones. "Hi, I'm Dave."

He guided me up a steep set of stairs and down a narrow hallway, where he showed me the room. It was a single room about six feet wide by twelve feet in length. There was a tiny closet, just big enough for a few pairs of pants and a couple of shirts. Just outside the door and to the left was a galley kitchen, and beyond that was a three-piece bathroom with a stand-up shower. "I'll take it."

It was a real shithole, but compared to where I'd been for five years, it was an upgrade. The condition of this domicile was no doubt the reason for there being no credit check. *Thank you, Lord!*

With Mom's help, I furnished my new digs with a used mattress I purchased at a local thrift store. They didn't have any box springs, so I laid a sheet of plywood under the mattress on top of the frame. My aunt worked at Walmart, and we used her employee discount to save me some money on all the things I'd need and want to be comfortable: a coffee maker, TV, DVD player, toaster oven, TV stand, mini fridge, and an area rug to lay over the disgusting floors that I couldn't scrub clean. I think my total bill came to about $500. After buying a phone, getting my driver's license, and setting up the apartment, I was left with a solid $4,000 in the bank. I could comfortably sustain myself for a long time if need be now. I was relieved to have a permanent address that was good enough to satisfy my PO's minimum standards, and thanked the Lord for providing for me.

It wasn't until the day we were moving my stuff into the new place that we realized my apartment was directly next door to the fire station. The loud blast of sirens announced this fact to us as we climbed the stairs with arms full of boxes. I stopped on the stairs to look back at my mother, and we exchanged looks. You can imagine the looks. Funny enough, within a week, I was so used to the sounds that I was only aware of it when someone else pointed it out, like The Brain when he came to visit. "What the hell is that?" He gasped while in my apartment. "You get used to it," I told him.

Once my week of "relaxation" was over, I hit the ground running. My first choice of employment was to be a trainer. I had helped so many "fat bastards," as Kim liked to call us, transform their bodies, it really made me feel good, and if I could earn a living doing that, I wanted to continue doing it. So, I took my newly minted fitness trainer certificate to the nearest gym and introduced myself to the owner.

"Hi, my name is Kevin. I'm new to town and I'm looking for work as a fitness trainer." I began to pull out my credentials but was stopped dead by his response.

"We don't need any more damn trainers! We got them coming out of our ears!" "Oh well, perhaps you have openings in machine maintenance, I have several years' experience in working on—"

"Nah, we have a service for that."

"Oh, um, okay," was all I could muster in my defeat.

I soon found out that the only other gym in town was the YMCA, and they did not offer any trainer services, and we're not interested in starting. Nor did they have any openings of any kind.

I knew I faced an uphill battle, so I didn't let my first two attempts get me down. I headed over to the Employment Security office to see what services they could offer. There I met a woman named Helen, who not only helped me get logged into their computer system where I was able to search through different job listings, but also gave me many tips on how to handle interviews: Things like being honest but brief while explaining my criminal past. Also what to write on applications when it comes to the question of felony convictions. She was an amazingly helpful and sweet lady, one I was glad to have met.

I left there having applied for several jobs online, and with a list of a few places I had to apply in person for, including one that I had to call to set up an interview. Thankfully, my mom worked the night shift, and she was able to drive me to the places that were out of the way during the day and would've taken me forever to get to by bus or by foot.

Our first stop was at a brick factory building for a job that was titled "Torque Tube Setup." What that was, I had no idea, and the job description was equally as vague. It read something like, "Job duties include making sure appropriate work is completed on time, adhering to all the company's standards for safety and quality, blah, blah, blah." Nothing that gave me any indication at all of what the actual job I would be expected to perform was. There were hardly any windows in the building, and the ones they had were either frosted or tinted.

Mom waited in the car while I found my way into a small, dark lobby. There was no receptionist, just a couple of chairs and a coffee table. Still there were no clues as to what this company was, or what they manufactured. On the counter I found a rack of resumes and a cup of pens. There was a sign that read, "After completing your application, dial 5263 and someone will be with you shortly."

I filled out the application, and when I got to the question, "Have you ever been convicted of any misdemeanors or felonies?" I wrote "Yes, will explain at interview," just as Helen had instructed me to do. It felt weird writing that, almost like a cop out. Like I was being evasive. However, I trusted my advisor and left it to fate.

I completed the application and called the number on a phone that was mounted to the wall. A few minutes later a woman appeared on the other side of a glass door, swiped her badge to unlock it, reached her hand through the partially opened door and snatched the paper. "We'll be in touch," was all she said as the door closed, and I watched her walk away back into the depths of the mystery building.

When I got back into the car, Momma said, "This is it. This is the job you're going to get. I have a feeling." She frequently had these "feelings" and has a fairly good track record of being right, but I was dubious.

"Mom, I don't even know what they do in there. I didn't even get to talk to anyone. The lady just took my application without so much as a hello."

"Nope, this is it," she said with a look of having inside information.

"Okay, but I think I'd better keep looking just in case."

From there, we went home so I could call some numbers I'd gotten from the Employment Security office. The first one was to a cleaning and janitorial business, where I was able to set up an interview immediately. I had done this kind of work before and was familiar with the high rate of turnover in the workforce and figured this to be true for this outfit as well, given the speed at which they wanted me to interview.

Mom and I drove to the next town over where I met with John and Abigail in their home while Mom waited in the car. There was a pickup in the driveway with a "T-Rex Janitorial" magnet on the doors. They both greeted me at the door along with a couple of barking dogs and three toddlers, who were spirited youths to say the least.

After we had exchanged greetings and Abigail had corralled the chaos of kids and dogs to another part of the home, we all sat down at their kitchen table to talk.

"Here's my resume," I began as I handed it over to John. He perused it while I continued, keeping the tips Helen had given me in the forefront of my mind. "What's not in my resume is the fact that I worked for a janitorial service for about one year, back in the nineties. It's not in my resume because I just put the most recent work history down."

"Oh, that's fantastic. What did you do specifically at that job?"

"Well, I took care of a grocery store and a drug store. I would arrive at the grocery store at eleven at night. I would sweep the entire store, then run the scrubber machine after that. Also, I had a schedule where I would strip sections of the floor, then re-wax them. So basically, over the course of each month the floors would be stripped and waxed completely."

"Wow, I'd love to get a grocery store," was John's only comment.

"Then," I continued, "at about four in the morning I would head over to my drug store where I would start the process all over again for them. The only difference being that in this store I would also run a buffer and clean and sanitize the bathrooms."

"Wow, that's great. It says here you've been working for the last five years as a fitness trainer?" John inquired. This was it, make it or break it, I knew.

"Yes. Now I want to be completely transparent about this job. I worked six days a week at this job. Eight hours Monday through Friday and four hours every Saturday. I trained people in group class settings, developed class programs, and taught nutritional and wellness classes. However, this job was in a prison, where I was an inmate. I had gotten myself mixed up in drugs, had gotten caught, and served my time. Honestly, it was the best thing that could've happened to me. It was a real wake up call, and it gave me the time to really examine my life and make the changes I needed to make to become a better person." John and Abigail sat slack-jawed while I prattled on, the feeling of cold sweat beginning to pool in my underarms and lower back. "I used the time to take substance abuse classes, all sorts of educational classes offered by the local community college, expand my spiritual horizons and, of course, get into fitness. I went into prison weighing 260 pounds and ate nothing but garbage. So, it was a total mind, body, and spirit transformation."

"Wow, I never would have guessed just looking at you," was Abigail's response, one that I'd be hearing many times to come.

"Well listen, I know it's a lot to consider, and I wouldn't blame you if you decide to pass on giving me a chance, but if you do give me a chance, I'll knock your socks off. I've got a hunger and a desire to make something of my life that I doubt many have." This got me a promising raising of their eyebrows.

Finally, I hit them with the only other incentive I had. "Also, if it helps, I have this pamphlet from the IRS. It gives you a tax credit of $1,700 if you were to hire an ex-felon." I handed over the flyer. They looked a little dumbfounded, but politely said they would consider it, and get back to me within a few days.

We said our goodbyes, and I headed out to the car. "How'd it go, honey?" Mom asked as she started the car and began backing out of the driveway. Before I could answer we heard hollering. "Hold up, stop!" Mom hit the brakes, and we rolled down our windows. John came trotting up to Mom's window. "Hi there, I'm John," he introduced himself. "I'm Linda, nice to meet you," she replied happily. John leaned down to face me through the window. "We talked about it, and we're just so impressed with you, and we have such a good feeling about this, that the job is yours if you want it."

So, there I was, employed on my first day of looking! The job was part time and paid $10 an hour. I went to work at seven o' clock at night to our local Honda dealership, where I spent four hours a night, five days a week cleaning bathrooms, vacuuming carpets, emptying trash cans, and cleaning and polishing the showroom floors.

I had only been working the janitorial job a few days when I got a call from UPS. I had applied there online my first day at the Employment Security office. They had me go in for an interview, and once again I employed the same upfront and totally transparent approach when it came time to explain my work history and criminal past. Once again it was a hit. "Oh, my goodness, I never would've guessed to look at you," the woman who did my interview told me.

I was offered a job on the spot, providing there were no surprises in my criminal history, other than that which I had explained. I told her I honestly couldn't reminder every conviction, but they were all drug related, and no sex or violent crimes of any kind. That was good enough for her.

I say I was offered a job, but actually I was offered a choice of two jobs. The first was a temporary driver's position which paid $22 an hour. I declined this one because they couldn't guarantee that I wouldn't have to travel outside of my state, which would be a violation of my probation, and because I didn't like the "temporary" nature of the work. Also, that job did not offer benefits, as I would've been a contractor instead of an employee. The job I took was a part-time truck loader. This worked out well because it started at four in the morning, and went to about nine, depending on the day. It paid just $8.50 an hour, quite a lot less, but the benefits were free to me, and there was not even a co-pay! So, I wouldn't have to quit my other job, and between the two incomes, I could afford to live in my little apartment and make all my bills.

On my first day on the job at UPS, the woman who did my interview pulled me aside, "Kevin, I just wanted to let you know that your background check came back clean."

"Oh, you mean nothing other than what I told you would be there?"

"No. I mean there was no criminal history whatsoever."

"You might want to hire a different firm to look into these things for you."

So now my daily routine was to go to the dealership and work until about eleven. I would go to my apartment, sleep for a few hours, get up and go to my second job before heading to Mom's to return her car. She would drive me home where I would once again sleep for as long as I could.

I had been keeping that schedule for about two weeks before I got a call from Timken, the mystery factory job I had applied for on my first day of job hunting. "We'd like to have you come in to take an aptitude test and do an interview," the woman told me over the phone.

On the day of my test and interview, I made my way to the waiting room where I'd first filled out my application. My mother's words came to mind as I entered the building, "This is it." I'm always early, so I found a chair and waited. Cell phone technology had yet to progress to the point where you could scroll the internet or Facebook in downtime yet. So, I just rehearsed my criminal history speech in my head, which seemed to be working like a charm. It was honest, so it wasn't hard to remember.

A few other applicants began to arrive, a Black fellow named Dwayne, a Hispanic man named Juan, and a White woman in her fifties named Charlotte. All their names I learned as I introduced myself when they arrived. We were a diverse group; I wondered if they were trying to fill a quota of some sort.

A woman opened the door and introduced herself to us. "Hi, I'm Brooke. If you all could follow me, I'll take you to the training room." Just then, a final applicant arrived, bursting through the door, slightly out of breath. She was a cute girl, about thirty years old. She had the look of someone who was used to being late. In fact, I knew she was often late, because I'd seen her at several NA meetings, and she was always late. Lisa was her name, and she wore jeans and a black zip up hoodie, and her hair was wet. Clearly, she had been rushing to make her appointment. I glanced at my watch and saw that she was three minutes late. I gave her a smile as she breezed past me to follow Brooke to a conference room.

We all settled into seats at tables that faced the front of the room where Brooke stood ready to address us. I was disappointed that Dwayne snatched the seat next to Lisa, as I was hoping to make a connection. But I wasn't here to find a date, after all.

Brooke had us take several timed tests that varied from basic math to mechanical situations, like if a line was run through a group of pulleys, which way would each pulley turn? It wasn't hard, although I could hear Charlotte muttering frustration under her breath.

About an hour later, Brooke announced we were finished with our testing. "Kevin and Lisa, I'd like you two to head across the street to Plant Two. You can go in the front door and have a seat. Someone will come to get you for an interview shortly. The rest of you can wait here and you'll be met by some folks here in Plant One for your interviews."

Lisa caught up with me as we were headed out the front door. "Do you want a ride?" she asked with that cute face looking up at me. I glanced across the street at Plant Two, literally a thirty second walk. "Yes, I would love a ride."

She wasted no time getting the conversation going once we were in her car. "You got plans after this?" she asked as she started the engine.

This is amazing I thought. *I'm not usually one that is good at picking up signals from women who are interested in me, but I was receiving this one loud and clear!* "Nope, I'm free. What do you have in mind?"

"We'll think of something," she told me with a mischievous grin as she pulled out of the first parking lot, crossed the street, and parked in the second.

We made some small talk on our way into the building. What was said between us I can't remember because I was in my head thinking how great it was that a girl this attractive was actually coming on to me.

We had only just sat down in the glass enclosed vestibule when a door to the inner building opened. There stood a disheveled man in his mid-fifties, with graying hair, wearing a wrinkled dress shirt that was only partially tucked into his waistband. He seemed unenthused as he peered over his reader glasses. "Mr. Gilford, come with me please." I got up to follow him. "I'm Peter, the supervisor here in primary turn," he said over his shoulder as we walked to his office.

We arrived at his office after a few twists and turns through cubicles and past photocopiers. He took a seat at his desk, and I sat in a chair next to it. It was a cramped affair, cluttered with stacks of paperwork piled on his desk and on top of two file cabinets that blocked most of the light coming through his lone frosted window.

The interview lasted all of about five minutes. Peter never looked up from my application and resume as I answered his questions, and I didn't get so much as a raised eyebrow when I delivered my speech about my criminal past, and all the work I'd done to better myself.

"Okay then. I've got another interview; we'll be in touch," he said as he rose from his chair and led me back to the vestibule. He held the door open for me and I was hit with a powerful scent of seductive smelling perfume that wasn't there before. I looked at Lisa who had removed her hoodie, revealing a deep V-neck shirt that showed an ample amount of cleavage. *Oh, she's a wily one all right!* Peter seemed to suddenly come to life. "Hello there, my name is Peter! Won't you please come this way?" he said with all the glee of a kid in an amusement park. Lisa handed me her keys as she walked past and whispered, "Wait for me in my car?"

I went to her car, sure of two things: one, that I wasn't the one who would be getting this job, and two, that I would be getting laid! It was a hell of a consolation prize. Plus, I already had two jobs that paid the bills, so I wasn't even mad.

As the minutes ticked by, I busied myself with inspecting the contents of her car. You know, to get a better idea of who I was getting involved with. Okay, let's call it what it was—snooping. I started with those things that were visible, a cigarette pack laying on the center console. I'd quit the habit years ago, but it wasn't a deal breaker for me. A pack of gum and some empty wrappers. There were some receipts and fast food bags littering the floorboards. *Not the neat and tidy type, okay, I could live with that too.* Inside the glove box I found makeup, tissues, and condoms. *Good, she's not going to give me any STDs!* I took the liberty of pocketing one of the condoms, closed the glovebox, then thought better of it and grabbed one more.

I started to take a tally of all the pros and cons; she's a bit of a slob, and she smokes cigarettes. She's constantly late, and clearly promiscuous. However, she's hot, she practices safe sex, and I first met her in NA meetings, so she must be trying to live a better life. Plus—and most importantly—she's made it clear that she's totally into me!

Thirty minutes must have passed before I saw Lisa emerge from the building. She had a spring in her step, and she did a little victory dance in front of the car for me. She slid into the driver's seat, then leaned over and kissed me on the lips. "I got the job in case you couldn't tell! Let's go celebrate!"

"My apartment is just down the street. It's pathetically tiny, but it's clean," I offered. She shifted back in her seat, raised her right leg onto the center console and lifted her pant leg, revealing an ankle monitor. "We have to go to my place, court orders. I have a bottle of tequila and some beers; we'll have a blast!" My heart sank. I'd already had not only the sex, but an entire relationship developing in my mind.

"I'm sorry, Lisa, but I can't do this." I could hardly believe the words coming out of my mouth. She looked as if I'd struck her in the face.

"What are you talking about, baby?" she asked, looking at me like I had a grotesque deformity.

"I'm on federal probation. I can't be around other convicts, and I certainly can't be drinking or with someone who is drinking." She faced forward and started her car. "Your loss, pal," she said flatly.

"Trust me, I know. This will haunt me for some time, I'm sure. Take care, Lisa," I told her as I exited the car. She immediately sped off, tires screeching as her car pulled out onto the road. *Discretion is the better part of valor*, I told myself in a weak attempt to console myself.

Later that same day, I got a call from Timken asking me to come in the next day for another interview. I was greeted in the lobby by a gentleman named Ron, who guided me to an office in the main building. He was a giant man with a stern face and a bald head. Though he was overweight, and about fifty, you could see that the majority of his weight was muscle. It was intimidating to say the least.

He sat across a desk from me and began in an almost accusatory manner. "What makes you want to work here, Kevin?" I wasn't expecting that question, but I plowed ahead, "Well Ron, honestly this was the first job I applied for when I got to town. The job description just said, 'Torque Tube Set Up and Operator, no experience necessary.' Until yesterday, I didn't even know that you manufactured ball bearings. But everyone I've talked to in this town says this is the best place to work if you want to make a career, and that most people that work here have done so for decades. I want to work for a place where I can make my mark, be given the opportunity for advancement, and God willing, retire from someday." That got me a raising of a singular eyebrow. *Good sign,* I thought. "Well, you don't have any experience in this field, but that could be a good thing. You don't have to un-learn any bad habits. It says here that you've been working as a fitness instructor for the last five years. Tell me about that." Ron pitched the ball back into my court. I launched into my speech looking him square in the eyes. "Well Ron, to be perfectly frank, that was the job I held in federal prison, where I was an inmate...." His expression did not change a fraction as I delivered my tale, but I didn't feel the cold sweats this time, and I felt much more relaxed telling my story than I had the first few times. After all, I was already employed, and I had nothing to lose.

When I'd finished, Ron paused a few moments, leaned back in his chair to level his gaze at me. "Well, that's fantastic! You'd never know it to look at you. I'm impressed with your honesty, and I can see that you'd be a good addition to the team. You've got the job," Ron stood and shook my hand in a vise grip.

Three jobs, all of which came from that first day's efforts! Mom was right after all. It was hard to let my boss at UPS know that I would be leaving so soon, but she understood. They couldn't compete with the $12 an hour and full-time status I had been offered. John and Abigail were much harder to tell that I was leaving. "I want you to know that I wasn't continuing to look for work after you hired me. This was actually the first job I applied for when I got to town," I'd explained. In the end, they were disappointed, but they understood. I continued to work for them until they found my replacement. It made for some exceedingly long days, but I owed it to them, and it made for some nice pay days.

I continued to journal long after my release. Sadly, those journals were accidentally thrown out long ago, but I do remember writing how I noticed that people love a comeback story. Everyone who's heard my story always seems to be genuinely happy to see the person I am now, and as I've pointed out, shocked that I lived the life I had. Being open and honest about my past was a hard thing for me to do at first. After my first prison bid, I would try and downplay the severity of my past and be guarded about letting too much information out. I constantly worried that I would be found out, and ruin relationships as a result.

Thanks to Helen at the Employment Security office who taught me to be open and honest at my interviews, now I live a life without fear of being found out, and everyone who has heard my story has expressed amazement at what I've been able to accomplish and been helpful in my journey. Helen did more than just help me to navigate an interview. She really helped me be a more authentic person in life.

I learned to stick to my principles! All my base instincts told me to go with Lisa that day. It had been five years, and until I'd gone to prison, I had not been without a woman in my life for more than a month or two. Of course, I had made the right decision, and it only took about a month to see how right I'd been. Lisa had quit her job, cut off her ankle monitor, and run off with some guy, only to be arrested trying to rob a bank in Vermont a short time later.

Chapter Twenty-Three
IN CLOSING

I've always said, going to prison was the best thing that could've happened to me. Before I went to prison, I was a slave to addiction to methamphetamines. It was an all-consuming entity in my life, nothing came before the drug. Not family, not bills, not work, and I would constantly betray my own sense of morality and values to feed my cravings.

Not only did going to prison remove me from having access to the drug, but it also gave me the time I needed to do a complete reset of my life. I had never been good at simple routines, like going to bed at an appropriate time so that I could wake up and get to work on time each day. Once I was forced into that simple schedule, I could then start to set goals that can only be achieved by slow and methodical work.

It also gave me perspective on what the really important things in life are: family, friends, community, and helping others. Before prison I was completely selfish. Everything had to be what I wanted, things had to go my way. I thought I could only be happy and content if it did. Now I find some of my greatest joys in life are when I can do something for someone else that brings them happiness or comfort.

I've heard many people who've been through what I have say that "I have no regrets, because everything that has happened brought me to where I am today and made me the person I am today." I've even said it myself. It's true that the journey was necessary, but I have many regrets. I've lied, cheated, and stolen from family, friends, and strangers alike so many times I couldn't possibly count. The torment I put my mother through, watching me throw my life away for so many years, still weighs on my heart. I moved three thousand miles away from my kids, trying to run away from my addiction (which doesn't work when you can manufacture your own drugs from scratch by the way)! I do have many regrets.

I thank God that today my family has found a way to forgive me and still loves me. Nothing brings me greater happiness than spending time with them and helping them when I can.

Memories of my past transgressions come to me every day. For a moment, when they come, I'm filled with disgust and shame. Yet I'm thankful for those memories because they serve as a stark reminder of who I was versus the person I am today.

I have found strength in my developing faith first. Mine is a classic found Jesus when I went to prison story. I wouldn't call myself religious by any means, but I found a faith, and it gives me strength and comfort to this day.

Getting healthy and losing weight was a process that gave me a lot of pride and satisfaction. I quit smoking and lost eighty-five pounds during my final prison stay. It was a journey that taught me a lot about setting goals and putting in the work on a daily basis to reach them. I struggle to this day with my weight, and as I write these words, I've gained thirty of those pounds back, but I have the roadmap on how to get back on track and I'm working towards that now.

Learning and expanding my education was another endeavor that gave me happiness while doing time. I took every class I could that was offered in the prison just to gather knowledge and expand my horizons. I took math, electrical, hazmat, and substance abuse courses to name a few. Some have been useful, and some have not, but the process helped me at the time, so in that way, I guess they were all useful.

My experiences have given me the confidence to face difficult situations that I would have cowered from previously. Once, when I was in a leadership position at my job, I was assigned a new manager, Mr. Rice. He had a reputation for being demeaning and aggressive to everyone he spoke to. It wasn't long before he tried that with me. I had been called into his office with a few of my crew members to account for a mishap that had happened in our department.

"What the hell were you thinking?" he yelled at me while we sat across from his desk. I calmly turned to my crew and said, "Gentlemen, please give Mr. Rice and I a few moments alone." They were glad to escape the situation and exited quickly. I rose from my chair and in a stern, but calm voice told him, "Don't you ever talk to me like that. I'm not some redheaded step-child of yours that you can just talk to anyway you please. I treat you with respect and I expect the same in return, savvy?" He was stunned, I doubt anyone had ever stood up to him like that before. He apologized for being out of line, not only to me, but my crew once they were invited back into the room. We went on to have a pleasant working relationship from that day forward. If I wouldn't let someone punk me out in prison, I damn sure wasn't going to let it happen for sixteen bucks an hour!

I never would've wound up with my wife had my life played out differently either. Though we still marvel at the fact that we did wind up together. She was raised a devout Catholic who'd never had a drug other than alcohol, let alone led a life of crime. The chorus of our song goes, "God bless the broken road that led me straight to you" which aptly describes our journey. I can at least partly attribute our relationship to my relatively newfound openness. She had been the friend of a girl I was interested in, and we had all spent lots of time together. I was incredibly open about my past, and she got to know me that way. When it didn't work out with the other girl, I asked her out. It took some persuading, but in the end, she said yes, and we couldn't be happier.

People can change, but only when they're ready. I wasn't ready until I was thirty-three years old. Some people are younger, some older, and sadly some never are ready. For me, I found that once I was making a concerted effort to change my own life, the opportunities were there, and people were accepting and helpful in my quest to make something of myself.

Since leaving prison I've done lots of things to try and be a positive contributing member of the society in which I live. I worked for a year volunteering at our local food bank, did annual trash pick-ups along roads and highways, and worked for Habitat for Humanity. I donate money every year to the United Way and other charities, served meals with my wife for seniors on Thanksgiving, and bought more raffle tickets to support charities than I can recall! (I've never won anything).

I swear I'm not trying to brag, just trying to underscore the fact that someone who at one time was always looking for ways to exploit others, did change, and is now always looking for ways to help others.

I have a million ideas of how I'd like to help in the future, most of which are somewhat grandiose and would require my winning the lottery (or maybe having a best seller), but I plan them out in my mind as if they will be happening someday. Ideas like building small homes to offer to people as rent-to-own properties. The idea here is that homeowners make for people who are more invested in their communities, but sadly so many folks suffer from bad credit, and low wages. My idea is to offer a pathway to home ownership to those who may not have that option otherwise, helping them to work towards a goal, and a better life where they can actually build some equity and security in their lives.

One idea is to build a relationship with probation and parole officers who may have that rare individual who is teetering on the brink of either making it or not. The kind of person that could really make something of themselves if they only had that one good break. My wife and I love renovating homes, and we no doubt would continue to do so even if we struck it rich. I can imagine taking on one of those souls and give them some work and some guidance from someone who's been where they're at in their lives and help to mentor them as they navigate the challenges they will face.

Could it sustain itself financially? Who knows, but there's a need, and I know retired folks have a wealth of knowledge and are often left feeling empty not being able to put their skills to use. A couple of extra bucks are always welcome to those in retirement as well, so it's a possibility.

So, if you're reading this now, you probably bought my book, and might just be helping me make some of these dreams a reality! So, thank you!

About the Author

Gilford, a current expert in manufacturing, has an outstanding life story that has looped and grumbled more times than your intestines after a bad dinner. Encouraged by friends and family to share his life story with others, he took the plunge in 2022 with his epic and jaw-dropping memoir, ***Everything I Ever Needed To Know About Life I Learned In Prison***. In his free time, the little of it that there is, he and his wife Cindy enjoy home renovations, hiking and spending time with family and friends.